# PSALMS
## *Songs of Dedication*

# PSALMS
## *Songs of Dedication*

*Volume 2*

PSALMS 51-100

*by*

ROBERT ALDEN

**MOODY PRESS**
**CHICAGO**

ISBN: 0-8024-2019-2

6 7 Printing/LC/Year 87 86 85 84

*Printed in the United States of America*

# INTRODUCTION

Within the group of Psalms 51-100 are some well-known ones. The very first, Psalm 51, is the classic Bible passage on repentance and rededication. Psalm 69 is a most insightful prayer by a suffering servant. The New Testament quotes several of its verses. The tender sentiments of Psalm 84 are especially beloved: "How lovely are thy dwelling places," and "A day in thy courts is better than a thousand." The prayer of Moses, Psalm 90, focuses on some of God's eternal attributes as no other portion of Scripture does. Psalm 91 is the source of the expression, "under the shadow of the Almighty." And Psalm 100 has been paraphrased into one of the most famous anthems in our hymn books.

All of these psalms were written by dedicated saints of old, motivated by the Holy Spirit. They display their love for God, their hatred of sin, their pain, and their joy. They have bared their souls to all who take time to read and study this very intimate part of God's Word.

The author's prayer is that his comments on these abiding songs of dedication will move people to true piety, biblical obedience, and fruitful service.

The well-known confession of David opens this second volume on the Psalms. Several phrases from Psalm 51 have etched their way into the thinking of haunted sinners who searched for words of regret and repentance. The tenth verse is perhaps the best known: "Create in me a clean heart, O God; and renew a right spirit within me."

The rather lengthy title to Psalm 51 provides a setting for the prayer. There is no reason to question the suitability of this confession for the situation. David's adulterous relationship with Bathsheba and his provision for Uriah's death are the blackest of scars on that godly king's character. In 2 Samuel 12 is recorded the encounter between Nathan, the reprimanding prophet of God, and the guilty king. This psalm, David's prayer to God for forgiveness, is in general enough terms so that all sinners, as well as sinning believers, may echo its sentiments.

The opening two verses contain four prayer verbs: "have mercy" and "blot out," "wash" and "cleanse." The first couplet (v. 1) is formed by the phrases "according to your lovingkindness" and "according to the multitude of your tender mercies." The second couplet (v. 2) has the parallel words "iniquity" and "sin." These are not two varieties of evil any more than God has two varieties of mercy. The concepts of God's grace and David's sin are intensified by the use of synonyms which help fill out the total picture. Verses 7 and 9 are similar to these opening two and will be considered in order.

Whereas verses 1-2 are essentially petition, verses 4-6 are basically confession. David acknowledges the several facets of the classic doctrine of sin, called hamartiology in theology texts. First he confesses in the most general terms that he has sinned. In the middle of verse 4 he defines sin. Sin is to do what is evil according to God. Apart from a standard of right, there can be no transgression of that standard (cf. Ro 4:15). Laws make criminals possible. God's holy Law, which demands perfection, makes us all sinners. Verse 4 concludes with a note of praise for God's justice.

Verse 5 points to the doctrine of total depravity. It does not state that David was the product of an illegitimate union. Traditional Protestant theology recognizes that all men are born sinners and that they all sin volitionally, as well. Here David recognizes these two aspects of guilt.

Verse 6 is another interjection of praise, while verse 7 picks up the petition for forgiveness begun in verse 1. Forgiveness involves two parties, the offender and the offended, the forgiven and the forgiver. The forgiven is restored to a place of joy and health (v. 8). The forgiving party—in this case, God—must put away the accusations. So verse 9 points to His part in this transaction. However, it is not until verses 16-17 that the price of pardon is mentioned.

The concluding four petitions (vv. 11-12) are in pairs, two negative and two positive. David prays *not* to be cast away and *not* to have God's Holy Spirit removed. Notice that "spirit" occurs in verses 10, 11, and 12. The "restore" and "uphold" of verse 12 indicate this is a believer's prayer. The unregenerate has never had the joy of salvation.

David promises to give God service (vv. 13-14). The sincerity of his confession, like the sincerity of ours, will be demonstrated by obedient service. Forgiveness is, in a sense, removal of the evil, but there must follow the execution of the good. These promises predate the Great Commission by 1,000 years; yet they underscore the great twofold task of the Church of Jesus Christ. We must bring sinners to the knowledge of God and we must praise God's righteousness. One can hardly be done without the other.

Furthermore, David recognizes that he needs divine enablement in this matter of witnessing. He prays what every hesitant Christian should pray: "Lord, open thou my lips."

The concluding verses (16-19) focus on the sacrificial system and its basic inadequacy. Like all perceptive Old Testament saints, David realized that God really did not want or need blood sacrifices as much as He demanded right attitudes which produced good deeds. The penitent must come not only with burnt offerings, but also with broken hearts. Repentance is more than doing penance. These well-known lines by Augustus M. Toplady express this truth:

> Nothing in my hand I bring,
> Simply to Thy cross I cling.

Good deeds must accompany good promises. The proof of David's sincerity would be his building the walls of Jerusalem. This divine-human intention he makes both a prayer to God and an instruction to himself and other confessors. Only as good behavior follows noble vows can any of the externals of the Old Testament religion be acceptable to God. Sacrifices of righteousness must bolster the offered bullocks. Otherwise the temple becomes merely a slaughterhouse and not the scene where men are reconciled to a holy and offended God.

## PSALM 52

The record of Doeg the Edomite's coming to Saul and announcing that David was at Ahimelech's house is in 1 Sam-

9

uel 22:9. It unfolds into a bloody massacre as Saul, jealous of David's growing popularity, has Doeg slay all the priests of Nob, including Ahimelech. Though no certainty should be attached to the titles of the psalms, this particular one is not at all unsuitable.

The "mighty man" of the opening verse is, then, King Saul. While he boasts in badness, God continues to deal with goodness. Apart from this initial reference to God's goodness (v. 1b), His loving-kindness does not appear until verse 8. The largest part of this complaint poem—first in a series that continues to Psalm 59—focuses on the wickedness and judgment of David's enemy.

The image of verse 2 likens the tongue to a razor: devising, deceiving, and cutting. The Revised Standard Version arranges the lines differently, effecting no basic change in meaning. The "all the day" of the newer scanning applies to the tongue's devising wickedness rather than to the loving-kindness of God.

A typical synonymous parallelism constitutes verse 3. Those who say *selah* means "think of that" have difficulty explaining why such an instruction should occur at the end of this verse. The Hebrew is better understood as some musical direction regarding volume, key change, posture, or antiphonal choirs.

Verses 2b-4 form a concise chiasmus. Note the deceitful tongue in the opening and closing lines, the word "love" in the intermediate parts, and the second half of verse 3 as the central stich.

The turning point comes with verse 5. Now the judgment of God and subsequent ridicule by the righteous are in view. This verse contains four varieties of punishment God will execute: He will destroy them; He will take them up; He will pluck them out; and He will root them from the land.

10

Verses 6-7 predict what the righteous will do when the wicked are judged. They shall learn the importance of reverencing God and His righteousness and rejoice that the wicked are punished. Rejoicing at the downfall of the wicked without fearing their own would leave out an essential. The punishment of criminals should serve to instruct the rest of the people. The opposite is an unfortunate modern phenomenon in America. Since many criminals go unpunished, fear of the law is lost. As a result, crime increases.

Verse 7 reads like an epitaph on the grave of an evil man. Rather than being strong in God, he was strong in wickedness.

The last two verses are the testimony of the good man, in this case, the righteous king of Israel. He chooses the green olive tree in God's house to illustrate life, productivity, and peace. Three vows sum up the characteristic attitude of this ancient God-fearer: "I trust," "I will give thanks," "I will hope" (MLB*). I recommend this last verse as a pattern for every Christian's outlook.

## PSALM 53

Psalms 14 and 53 are almost identical. Only the latter part of Psalm 53:5 varies from Psalm 14, and Psalm 14:6 is not found here. The title to Psalm 53 differs slightly too. It has the additional remarks, "set to Mahalath" and "a Maschil." *Mahalath* is perhaps a hymn tune or a musical instrument. It occurs again only in the title to Psalm 88. *Maschil,* a much more common word, is a kind of song.

*Modern Language Bible* (The New Berkeley Version in Modern English, rev. ed. [Grand Rapids: Zondervan, 1969]).

No explanation of why there are two copies of the psalm is satisfactory. We must simply understand that here are two redactions of the same work.

In addition to the differences noted above, it is interesting to observe that the name *God* is substituted for LORD (a characteristic feature of Psalms 42—72) in three places (vv. 2, 4, 6), while a fourth occurrence of the divine name in Psalm 14 is in the verse eliminated from Psalm 53. Other variations are even less significant.

While the commentary on Psalm 14 can be read for this psalm, additional remarks are appropriate for verse 5*b*. It is a picture of judgment—judgment on the enemies of Israel. Because they desired and demanded a decent burial, the scattering of bones may be among the worst threats of punishment. Recent archaeological finds have substantiated that many ancient peoples had second burials. Shortly after death, the entire body would be interred for a year or more. Only minimal preparation was done to preserve the corpse. Later the bones would be exhumed and put into a smaller casket, ossuary, or bonebox for permanent burial. Sometimes the bones were merely piled in a family cave. The disarray in which some skeletons were found points to such a second entombment.

The scene of Psalm 53:5*b* is that of God not giving an honorable second burial to His and His people's enemies, who are described in the body of the psalm as very godless.

In general, this and Psalm 14 are very gloomy. Only the last verse of each picks us up and makes us glad. With similar aspiration we ought to anticipate the joy of seeing God save and liberate those destined for His Kingdom.

# PSALM 54

Psalm 54 is a typical short "trouble and trust" song. Its format is that of a prayer but includes complaint to God about enemies, and rejoicing in their anticipated destruction. Several words occur more than once in its seven verses: "God" is twice in the vocative (vv. 1-2) and two other times in addition. "Thy name" occurs in verses 1 and 6. "My soul" appears in verses 3 and 4. There are five synonyms for trouble: two in verse 3, one in verse 5, and two in verse 7. No clear outline appears from noting these features.

According to the title, which comprises two verses in the Hebrew Bible, the setting for this psalm may be found in 1 Samuel 23—a chapter filled with intrigue as it recounts Saul's pursuit of David. David sought to evade Saul by hiding in the woods of Ziph. But the Ziphites were on Saul's side and betrayed David's hideout to jealous and angry King Saul. But, in a fashion similar to old-time radio serials, David was not there when Saul closed in for the kill. He had moved to another desert spot, which Saul in turn surrounded. Only the report of a new Philistine invasion decoyed Saul away, and the relieved David took the opportunity to retrench at En-gedi. The enemies to which David refers in this psalm, therefore, are Saul, his soldiers, and the Ziphite informants.

The opening two verses contain four imperatives which sum up the psalmist's request: "save me," "judge me," "hear," and "give ear." The word "judge" in this context means "to execute justice." David certainly would have won this contest in a court of law. Saul did not have a legal leg to stand on, and both he and David knew it. For that reason only, David pleads for a trial.

Notice once again the appeal to God's name and the parallel, God's strength. To the ancient Semite a name was more than a label or an identification tag; it was the person himself. To invoke a name was to invoke the person. The custom is preserved when we pray in Jesus' name.

Verse 3 delineates the reasons for the prayer. The Ziphites were strangers who for no reason cast their lot with wicked Saul rather than with righteous David. One could forgive Saul's soldiers for being loyal to their leader, but why should strangers who apparently have nothing to lose or gain, show such allegiance? In addition to seeking to kill David, they are also charged with godlessness. Even so today, violent people intent on murder cannot entertain God and His Law in their minds.

If verse 3 is the "trouble" part of this psalm, then verse 4 is the "trust." A *selah* divides this turning point. "Uphold my soul" may perhaps be translated as "sustain my life," the same life that the violent men (v. 3b) sought to destroy.

Having said what God would do for him, David continues to tell what God will do to his enemies (v. 5). They will be repaid and, he hopes, destroyed. God's truth or fidelity is not the instrument of their destruction but the reason for it. Because God knows who is guilty or innocent, He can, on the basis of that truth, execute justice.

The last two verses are somewhat of an epilogue. Already anticipating his vindication and his enemies' punishment, David promises to do his duty to God and express his gratitude with offerings. In the light of the discussion on the word "name" above, observe that he gives thanks to God's name, for He is good.

Verse 7 may refer to David's envisioning the answer to this prayer, or it may be a reflection on past deliverances. There is no spiritual therapy like counting blessings and ex-

14

pecting more. The account in 1 Samuel 23 records neither the first nor the last narrow escape David had. If God delivered His child before, will He not do it again? If He has let you see your enemy removed, will He not give you victory over any present or future difficulty?

## PSALM 55

The title to Psalm 55 gives no indication of the setting for the composition. We can only guess from the context. Verse 9 may give some indication that the treachery described occurred in an urban context; and verse 13 points out that a close friend turned against the psalmist.

In typical fashion the psalm begins with an invocation to God. After that two-verse introduction there follows complaint in the next three verses. All of the charges are in general terms and could describe any number of troubles David or other biblical saints, or even we, have experienced. The persecution seems to be mostly verbal abuse and threatened, rather than actual, physical harm. As we all know, words can sometimes injure more cruelly than inflicted blows. Whatever the nature of the enemy's attacks, they produce fear, trembling, and horror for the author.

Verses 6-8 probably speak for all of us at one time or another. When things grow bad, the urge to escape becomes much greater. Oh, to be like a bird and fly away from it all! Oh, to be far from the rat race of everyday life and tension to enjoy a cabin in the woods or a cave in the desert! Oh, to be out of the storm and in a safe and quiet shelter! And some Christians' professed love for the Lord's appearance is only a veiled wish for their own disappearance.

15

Despite the "selah" before verse 8, verse 9 begins a new section. In much the same manner as the psalm began, verse 9 is a prayer followed by complaints in the succeeding verses. It is not as if a new psalm begins, for this section refers to what precedes. The prayer is for destruction of the wicked tongue, that cruel agent which afflicts the psalmist. The prayer also mentions the violence of the city in contrast to the rest and peace available in the wilderness lodge. A description of the wicked city continues (vv. 10-11).

With verse 12 the psalmist starts to focus attention more particularly on his onetime friend, now turned enemy. A traitor is an especially bad enemy, for his enmity is not immediately suspected and certainly not anticipated. He shelters his evil intentions behind your friendship for him. Such treachery must have been perpetrated against the author of this psalm. He reminisces about the days when his friend and he went to God's house together, chatting as they went. But those days are gone forever. That one stab in the back proved what a false friend he was.

Do not mistake the "thou" to be God in verse 13. It is obvious from the grammar of verse 14 that this enemy is not God, though he has been referred to in both the second person pronoun (*you*) and the third person pronoun (*he*).

The balance of the psalm alternates between vindictive prayers for the enemy's destruction and testimonies of God's faithfulness. Here is the record of a man who simultaneously prays for calamity on his foes and blessing on himself, accuses them and defends himself, anticipates their punishment and his own exoneration, testifies to their deceit and his integrity.

The imprecatory verses are 15, 19, and 23. The blessing verses are 16-18, and 22. The prayed-down plagues are as severe as anything elsewhere in the psalms. For instance, note verse 15*b,* that the wicked might be buried alive; and verse 23*b,* that they should die before reaching middle age. Verses 20-21 comport with verse 13. It was an old friend who turned against him. The figures of verse 21 are quite vivid. The traitor had a mouth and words like butter and oil but, swordlike, they veiled a heart at war.

On the other hand, the confessions of trust and the notes of praise are as sweet as the complaints were bitter. In spite of the accusations, and beyond the troubles, there is God. And according to verse 16, He will save. Additional thanks for deliverances are in verse 18.

The injunction to us, the modern readers of this ancient literature, is verse 22. This is the lesson the twentieth-century saint can learn from a work such as this. "Cast your burden on the LORD, and He will sustain you; He will never allow the righteous to be shaken" (NASB*). The time may come in our lives when a close friend, perhaps even a relative, will turn against us, pull out the carpet, so to speak, and maybe even thirst for our blood. While we pray that such a thing will never happen, let us be prepared to echo the words that close this psalm: "I will trust in Thee."

## PSALM 56

Psalm 56 is another in the series of "trouble and trust" psalms, a series extending from Psalm 52 through Psalm 59. It follows the format of others with these various elements: invocation, complaint, supplication, anticipated destruction of enemies, and anticipated bliss and vindication for the psalmist. The order may vary from psalm to psalm,

*New American Standard Bible (Chicago: Moody, 1973).

17

and some features may be repeated or slighted, but generally these themes characterize this type of psalm.

The title is taken with varying degrees of seriousness or authority. Part of the reason is the uncertainty of some of the words, and part because the antiquity of the titles is questionable. Several translations of the tune to which this psalm is set are possible and can be found in modern versions, while the old versions simply transliterate the Hebrew words.

The account of David feigning insanity (1 Sa 21:10-15) fits the historical note in the title. But, like many other psalms, the content is very unspecific and suits many instances in David's life and the lives of others.

The invocation of this poem is very brief—merely the first stich of verse 1. Immediately the writer launches into his complaint over his enemy, which is sometimes singular and sometimes plural. In fact, the same verb, "swallow," comes in verses 1 and 2. The phrase "daily" (or, "all [the] day long") also appears in these two verses. The verb "fight" also occurs twice. If, indeed, David is the author and it was written on the occasion of his flight from Saul to the inhospitable Philistines, the singular enemy might be the first king of Israel, and the plural enemy the Philistine lords.

From the despair of verse 2 the psalmist turns to the confidence of verse 3. Again notice the repetition of the words "trust," "in God," and "afraid." Such repetition as occurs in verses 3-4 and in verses 1-2 is typical of ancient Semitic poetry. It does not indicate a small vocabulary but is a device to impress certain concepts on the reader. Reiterating the same words in different phrases is like viewing a jewel from several angles. For instance, verses 3-4 could be summarized: "When I am afraid, I will not be afraid."

The alternate theme of complaint takes the stage in verses

5-6. Once more the expression "every day" (or, "all [the] day long") occurs. These two verses focus on the manner of the attack more than on the simple fact of it. The foe has plotted to ambush the righteous man.

In the middle of verse 7 the complaint gives way to imprecatory prayer. This half verse is the only section of the psalm that can be labelled as prayer against enemies. Complaint and anticipated destruction appear later on. But, unlike some of the psalms, the actual calling down of a curse is relatively brief.

Self-pity is the essence of verse 8. Though there is some question regarding the meaning of "bottle," whether it is a wineskin or simple parchment, the point is clear. God keeps a record of all things, and to that record the psalmist appeals in verse 9. He knows that, on the day the books are opened, God will justify him and condemn his oppressors.

Because verses 10-11 are so similar to verse 4, a hint of the strophic structure of the composition may be present. The answer to the rhetorical question in verse 11 is "nothing." Man can do nothing to the eternal hurt of one who trusts in God. As in several preceding psalms (51:19; 52:9; 54:6) there is the promise to thank and bring offerings for the anticipated deliverance.

A better understanding of Hebrew syntax and the way speech, both ancient and modern, works makes unnecessary the several italicized words in verse 13 (KJV,* ASV†). A simple interrogative article is attached to the negative, and most accurately it should be translated "No?" or "Isn't it so?" and read with the inflection to indicate the preceding is definitely true. Hence: "You delivered my life from death and my feet from falling. No?"

*King James Version (Authorized Version).
†American Standard Version (1901).

19

The psalm closes with a happy benediction which looks forward to a long, godly life. As long as we can see beyond our troubles—those enemies of our souls—to the vindicating, all-righteous God, we will come out spiritually on top. Generally it takes little calculation to see that God's blessings far outweigh the temporal trials that plague us.

## PSALM 57

A refrain in verses 5 and 11 divides Psalm 57 into two stanzas or strophes. The first stanza contains prayer and complaint in that order (vv. 1-4). The second stanza contains complaint and promise in that order (vv. 6-10). So there is a rudimentary chiasmus within the total psalm. The composition fits into this series of laments or "trouble and trust" psalms, as we call them.

Again the title focuses on a specific incident (cf. 1 Sa 22:1), but the generalities in the psalm make it applicable to various episodes in the lives of many different persons. The words transliterated from the Hebrew as *Al-taschith,* mean "destroy not" (see MLB and RSV*), and may be cited from Deuteronomy 9:26, where Moses prayed that God would not destroy His people after the incident of the golden calf.

The psalmist is moderate in that he does not get to his complaint for several verses. The first three verses are entirely prayer. Perhaps we could learn from this approach. Which is bigger, our problem or our God? Do we stop to recognize who He is with whom we have to deal before we clutter His audience hall with the trivia of our faithless lives?

*Revised Standard Version (New York: Oxford, 1962).

The initial supplication, "be merciful," occurs twice (v. 1). Not until verse 5 is there another imperative. Rather, the psalmist asserts his confidence that God will protect and bless. The illustration of verse 1 is of a mother hen comforting and protecting her brood. God does not have wings, but He does provide for our physical and psychological needs.

The last stich of verse 1 and the middle stich of verse 3 only hint at the trouble. Not until the fourth verse do the enemies come into full view. They are like lions. They burn with passion. They have teeth like spears and arrows, and a tongue like a sharp sword. Perhaps no physical harm has yet befallen the writer of this complaint, but the threats are abundant and frightening. Therefore he complains primarily about their teeth and tongues rather than their actual swords and arrows. A benediction closes the first stanza.

The second stanza begins, without hesitation, to outline more of the troubles of this ancient saint. A net was spread and a pit was dug, but the devices produced an unexpected result—the wicked trapped themselves.

Once the initial verse of complaint in this stanza is passed the remainder is praise and promise. From a steadfast heart the psalmist promises to sing God's praise. He summons various musical instruments to assist. Psalm 150 gives more explanation of the musical instruments. We would probably not find such music too pleasing since most of the instruments were percussion and strings. Most likely the music was loud and rhythmic—even shattering.

Verses 9-10 are perfect examples of Hebrew parallelism. The psalmist thinks as high and wide as he can—to the (foreign) nations and peoples, and to the heavens and skies.

The refrain of verse 5 closes the work: "Be thou exalted, O God, above the heavens: let thy glory be above all the earth."

# PSALM 58

Except for the lack of a historical note, the title to Psalm 58 is identical to the superscriptions of Psalms 57 and 59. Psalm 58 is more caustic in its charges against the wicked than the preceding psalms. It also contains some very difficult Hebrew.

The general outline divides the psalm at verse 6. The first half is a charge against the wicked; the latter half is an imprecatory prayer for their destruction. Evidence of chiasmus is present in the repetition of various words. Concepts of righteousness and justice occur in the first and last verses. The same Hebrew word for wicked appears in verses 3 and 10. Verses 2 and 10 may be linked with the terms "hands" and "feet." Both verses 3 and 8 have the idea of birth in them, though identical Hebrew words are not used. There may be a connection between the snakes of verse 4 and the snail of verse 8, although the latter is one of the questionable words. Lastly, in the middle verse a parallel exists between "teeth" and "fangs" (v. 6, NASB).

The first difficulty arises with the second word (in Hebrew) of the psalm. The King James Version renders it "O congregation"; the American Standard Version, "in silence"; the New American Standard Bible, "O gods"; and the Modern Language Bible, "O you judges." I propose *to them,* although there is no antecedent. The meaning is clear as soon as the second half of the verse is read: "Do you judge the children of men fairly?" (MLB).

The vicious indictment continues through verse 2. Their wickedness takes two steps: first the plot is worked out in their hearts, and then it is executed with their hands.

The psalmist switches to the third person in the next six

verses. Though Psalm 51:5 is not part of this series and is in a much different context, it states the same truth.

Verses 4-5 go together and describe the wicked in terms of a venomous serpent. Unlike serpents, which are obedient to their charmers (a word found only once in the Hebrew Bible), they cannot be made to reason or submit. The enemies of the righteous are as untrustworthy and deadly as poisonous reptiles.

The imprecatory prayer begins in verse 6 with two parallel wishes for broken teeth. Perhaps the first teeth belong to the poisonous serpents of the preceding verse (5) and the second teeth belong to the lion of the last half of verse 6. Teeth in particular and other parts of the mouth in general occur in nearly every psalm in this series (cf. Ps 52:2; 53:4; 55:21; 56:1-2; 57:4; 59:7, 12).

Verses 7-9 are as difficult and uncertain of interpretation as any part of the Psalms. Some words are certain but are in contexts with other words which may be unknown or do not fit well. The number of italicized words in the King James Version gives some indication of the difficulty. Perhaps the biggest problem is our lack of understanding of ancient figures of speech. Whole volumes are given to the study of Semitic curses, and these four or five curses belong among them. Because they are proverblike, they are difficult to translate or even understand. Think of the difficulty a foreigner must have understanding some of our expressions such as, "He had to eat crow or his name would be mud."

At least there is some consensus on the first half of verse 7. The psalmist wishes the wicked to disappear like water into the sand, an action which the word "melt" could describe. All agree that verse 8 seems to be praying that the wicked will miscarry their babies.

With verse 10 the translation is easier and the point quite

23

clear. When the wicked are punished, the righteous rejoice. The gruesome figure of bathing feet in blood is better tolerated when we remember the age when this poetry was written—an age of bloodshed, violence, physical cruelty, and revenge.

Having been vindicated, the protagonist praises God for His justice. The enemy has received his due and the righteous his reward. Such satisfaction of justice prompts the closing expression, "Verily he is a God that judgeth in the earth."

Christians might well meditate on the conclusion, rather than study the curses. David did not have the beatitudes of the pattern of Jesus' life to follow. We do.

## PSALM 59

Psalm 59 is the third *michtam* in a row set to the same tune. It is the last in a series of seven or eight psalms of complaint against enemies, called "trouble and trust" or "lament" psalms.

Again certain themes prevail: prayer for personal deliverance, imprecation on the foes, complaint, description of the enemy, and promises to praise. The verses which focus on the enemy are interwoven with verses of petition to God for the enemy's destruction and the psalmist's deliverance. The verb "defend" ("set on high," ASV) and the cognate noun "defense" ("high tower," ASV) tie together the latter group of verses (1, 9, 16, 17). Notice also the repetition of verse 6 in verse 14. A *selah* precedes both.

In typical fashion, the psalm begins with four imperatives: "deliver me," "defend me," "deliver me," and "save me." Likewise the foe is described in four ways: "mine enemies," "them that rise up against me," "the workers of iniquity," and "bloody men."

The description of the enemy's activities begins in verse 3 and continues on and off through verse 15. In addition to the complaint, a protest of self-righteousness is present in verses 3-4. The psalmist wants to underscore his enemy's guilt and his own innocence. Such a tactic is all right, providing it is true.

The second half of verse 4 starts another series of demands on God. Two of the requests are antithetically parallel: "awake to help me" and "arise to visit all the heathen." If these two elements are labeled A and C, then the remaining two, B and D, have a militaristic tone: the God of military powers ("hosts") must not have mercy on wicked transgressors.

The first occurrence of the refrain, if we might call it that, comes in verse 6. The picture of a pack of howling, belching dogs roaming the city streets is not a pleasant one, but neither were these enemies very pleasant. With all respect to modern dog lovers, ancient peoples had little use for dogs. Their only contribution was to scavenge refuse and bark at intruders.

Verse 8 is similar to Psalm 2:4.

The halfway point is marked by a note of praise quite similar to the closing verse of the psalm.

Again (v. 11) the cursing of the enemy resumes. If the first word of verse 11 in Hebrew is read differently, it can mean, "O God, slay them" rather than "slay them not."

The complaint of verse 12 centers on the words of the enemy's mouth rather than on their actual deeds. Another

25

series of curses follows, beginning with "consume them" (v. 13) and ending with "let them wander" and "be not satisfied." The "dog" refrain comes at verse 14, and the curses of verse 15 sustain the figure of hungry, roving packs.

A promise and a benediction close the psalm. Elements from earlier verses echo in this optimistic conclusion. The note of mercy ("lovingkindness," NASB) is first struck in verse 10. The high tower ("defence") is in verse 9. "His [God's] strength" also occurs in verse 9. Perhaps the "morning" of verse 16 is in contrast to the "evening" of verses 6 and 14.

All of the psalms in this series, given over to complaints and curses against enemies, end on notes of praise. We all go through times of mental anguish when we wonder if God exists or hears us, or is helping our enemies, and His. We all secretly wish their demise and our own vindication. But let us not stop there. Let us with these ancient psalmists bring our experience to the blessed and hopeful conclusion that ends each of these psalms. Despite circumstances, do not forget, "God is my high tower, the God of my mercy" (ASV).

## PSALM 60

In the course of expanding his kingdom, David must have experienced some setbacks. Psalm 60 reads like a national lament over a defeat in battle. The title points to 2 Samuel 8 and 1 Chronicles 18. David conquered the countries mentioned but perhaps suffered some reverses before victory was accomplished. Though the psalm is a lament, it is also a prayer for help and a song of hope. The first half of verse 1 is the same as verse 10a, which may mark the beginning of a new strophe. Verses 5-12 are almost identical to Psalm 108: 6-13, with a "selah" at the division point.

Verses 1-4 are the heart of the lament. The defeat in battle is likened to a cosmic catastrophe and blamed on God, who has left their ranks. No reason ever appears why such a reverse should occur, and there is no repentance on the part of the king or the people. Verse 2 describes the calamity in terms of a violent earthquake. Notice that interspersed in the lament are brief petitions for help: "restore us again" (v. 1, ASV) and "heal the breaches" (v. 2, ASV).

As in other passages, God's wrath or discipline is pictured as a drink to be imbibed by the afflicted (cf. Ps 75:8; 51:17; Jer 25:15; Mt 20:22).

Verse 4 is difficult to interpret in the light of what immediately precedes. The Greek translation gives a sarcastic sense: that the banner ordinarily used to rally to battle is raised for retreat. This is unnecessary if the verse is tied with what follows rather than with what precedes. Despite the present defeat, God has provided a rallying point. That banner is the encouragement of the oracle of hope (vv. 6-8). Its purpose is to deliver the beloved, probably meaning the king, with a play on words, since in Hebrew "David" is from the same root as the word "beloved."

Verses 6-8 and perhaps 9 contain the quotation of God's promise given in His holiness or in His holy sanctuary. As the Owner, He is free to parcel out Shechem and the valley of Succoth. Shechem was the outstanding city in the northern part of the country. The valley referred to may be the Jordan Valley, since Succoth has been tentatively located at a tell north of Jericho. Gilead and Manasseh are in northern Trans-Jordan. Ephraim is a major tribe in the north while Judah is the major tribe in the south, having in its bounds the capital city of Jerusalem. Moab, Edom, and Philistia are

27

neighbors to the east, southeast, and southwest, respectively. The strong city of verse 9 to which either the king or God wishes someone to bring him may be the famous rock city of Petra. The derogatory terms applied to Moab and Edom have several explanations. The shoe-casting (v. 8) may not refer to the refusal of terms, as in Ruth 4:7, but simply to walking over the land, which in this context means invasion.

The lamentation resumes (v. 10) with the words that opened the psalm. God has not accompanied the army into battle and this has brought defeat. The last two verses (11-12) are given over to supplication and prayer for victory. Human strength cannot save; only in God is there hope. Though the psalmist complains of being forsaken by God, he is not going to forsake God. He realizes there is no help except in God and that it would be sealing his doom to reject the only avenue of escape and the only source of physical and spiritual salvation.

## PSALM 61

A confession of trust and prayer for or by the king comes in Psalm 61. In verses 1-5 the supplicant is "I," but from verse 6 on the third person is used. Perhaps the king, even David, refers to himself in this detached style (vv. 6-7).

The superscription indicates that the psalm is for or of the chief musician, played perhaps on a stringed instrument called a *Neginah*. It is for, or by, or of David. The same preposition precedes the chief musician as precedes David. The enigmatic "selah" divides the work exactly in half, rather than at the point where the object shifts from "me" to "him."

The opening verse is the invocation in a typical synonymous parallelism, with similar verbs ("hear" and "attend unto") and similar direct objects ("my cry" and "my prayer").

Some have inferred from "the end of the earth" that the speaker is in exile in some distant country. On the other hand, the reference to a high rock may indicate a desert exile such as David experienced in his flight from Saul. This verse prompted William O. Cushing to pen the well-known hymn, "Hiding in Thee." The opening lines read:

> O safe to the Rock that is higher than I,
> My soul in its conflicts and sorrows would fly.

Warrant for such an application is entirely scriptural (cf. Ps 18:2; 1 Co 10:4). The figure is especially vivid to someone who has spent time in a parched, waterless waste. Any rock large enough to offer shade from the scorching sun is welcome. The other noteworthy value of rock is for foundation and that may be the interpretation here as it certainly is in the psalm (v. 2) and in the parable of the wise man who built his house on a rock (Lk 6:48).

From the supplication of verse 2 the psalmist turns to testimony in verses 3-5. God is likened to four varieties of shelters. He is a refuge or fortress; He is a strong tower; He has been a tent for shelter and wings for covering. The tent or tabernacle may allude to the sanctuary of God on earth, or may simply be a figurative term for God's protection. The latter is probably better in this context.

One slight variation of interpretation is available in verse 5. Is it that God has given *to* the psalmist the heritage *of* those who fear His name? Or have *all* God-fearers received the heritage? On either interpretation, the point is that there is some distinct advantage to fearing the Lord, an advantage termed here as an inheritance or a heritage.

The king, who may be the speaker throughout the psalm, is mentioned as the beneficiary of God's blessing of long life (v. 6). Despite his many close calls, David did live to be seventy years old.

Verse 7 can refer to the afterlife. Thus the testimony is twofold: he will live a long life on earth and then forever after in God's presence.

The closing verse (v. 8) contains an interesting contrast between praising God forever and performing vows daily. Sometimes the long view obscures the immediate. It is a fine thing to focus on eternity, but the "here and now" is where and when we should be bearing spiritual fruit.

## PSALM 62

A mixture of themes is present in Psalm 62, but the overriding one is trust. Verses 1-2, 5-8, and 11-12 are three groups of assertions or recommendations of faith in God, who will protect and deliver. In fact, verses 1-2 are almost identical to verses 5-6. The remaining verses, 3-4 and 9-10, are complaints about the wicked and warning against wickedness. Grammatically speaking, every person, singular and plural, occurs in the psalm (I, thou, he, us, you, they). Sometimes it is difficult to know whom is being spoken to or about. In verses 1-2 the psalmist confesses to God. In verses 3-4 both the "you" and the "they" refer to enemies. Verses 5-7 are like verses 1-2, but verses 8-10 are exhortations directed to fellow believers. Mainly because of these three verses some call this a didactic or instructional psalm. Finally, the last two verses (11-12) have the psalmist as the subject and God as the object, except for the very first line of verse 11.

As noted in Psalm 39, Jeduthun was an official temple musician (1 Ch 16:41 f.; 25:1). Perhaps he wrote the music to which these words were sung. Again, the title does not help the understanding of the psalm. The terms are quite general and could be the experience of any number of different persons.

The statements are confessions of belief in one God. He is the salvation, the rock, and the high tower (ASV) of the poet. In verse 2 the "greatly" is difficult. Perhaps that modifier should be an adjective with "tower" rather than an adverb with "moved." Hence: "My great high tower; I shall not be moved."

The scene shifts (v. 3) and the remarks are addressed to violent men. Both the leaning wall and the tottering fence may be either the wicked man or the righteous whom he is oppressing. In verse 4, rather than being addressed, they are described as arch-hypocrites and liars.

An appropriate "selah" marks the division between verses 4-5 and 8-9. Another confession of trust begins this section using phrases almost identical with verses 1-2. The words "salvation" and "rock" echo again in verse 7. Verse 8 is still part of the positive section of the psalm, but its format is exhortation. The psalmist's contemporaries, or we, the readers, are urged to trust in God at all times. In form, verses 8 and 10 go together. The former is positive and tells us what to trust in, while the latter is negative and tells us what not to trust in.

Verse 9 intercepts the exhortation with a scathing description of the worthlessness of the wicked depicted by a vivid, everyday scene from ancient commerce. Put the wicked on a balance scale, and up they go for lack of worth. The Hebrew language, interestingly, builds the words for "curse" and "weightlessness" on the same root; "heavy" and "glorify" likewise share a common stem. Evangelists sometimes use this illustration. In one pan is the perfect God-man, Christ Jesus, and in the other the sinner and his meager self-righteousness. The result is that all come short of the glory of God (Ro 3:23; cf. Dan 5:27).

Verse 10 urges the saints not to trust in oppression, robbery, and riches. The order in which these appear may be significant. Ill-gotten gain will be of no avail when God weighs our merits.

The two concluding verses (11-12) are a kind of benediction. The "once-twice" sequence is a typical device found elsewhere in the Bible, but with different series of numbers. For "two-three," see Deuteronomy 17:6. For "three-four," see Proverbs 30:18, 21, 24, 29; Amos 1:3, 6, 9, 11, 13; 2:1, 4, 6. For "six-seven," see Proverbs 6:16. The modern English expression is, "If I've heard it once I've heard it a thousand times!" And we have. In capsule form the two major truths of the Gospel are summed up in verse 12. God is love, but God will also judge every man. How many times have you heard that? Once? Twice? A thousand times?

## PSALM 63

The title to Psalm 63 fits well with the contents. The wilderness of Judea is a "dry and thirsty land where there is no water." And the "king" (v. 11) might well be the psalmist speaking of himself in the third person (cf. Ps 61:6). The psalm speaks of the aspiration of the believer to be in God's presence. Except for verses 9 and 10 and the last line of 11, no negative note is sounded.

Verse 1 opens with a typical invocation: "O God, . . . my God." The verb "to seek early" is related to the noun for "morning" and can be taken with that obvious meaning. This initial confession is a case for morning devotions. Soul and body, he wishes to be in God's presence. Perhaps David was literally in the desert. We may experience dearths of fellowship and droughts of spiritual blessings. The opportunity for fellowship and the privilege of sharing with the gathered church are dearly missed when they are not available. There is no loneliness like that of the Christian in a strange and hostile world, unable to enjoy another believer's presence and comfort.

As in other places in the psalm and elsewhere, the word "sanctuary" may not refer actually to the yet-unbuilt Temple but to that retreat where God's holiness is to be found. Verse 2a makes commentators think this an exilic psalm with the speaker yearning to return to the holy city. I prefer the more general interpretation, that the psalmist longs to enjoy God's holiness, power, and glory whether on sacred Mount Zion or in the solitude of En-gedi.

The sentiment of verse 3 is highly exalted. To think of God's covenant fidelity, His loving-kindness, and His unfailing mercy as better than life indicates a spiritual plateau few reach. Paul was on that plateau when he said, "For me to live is Christ, and to die is gain" (Phil 1:21; cf. Ps 116: 15).

Having said that this life is secondary to enjoying God, David continues to vow that as long as he is alive he will bless God with uplifted hands (v. 4).

Verse 5 stands in contrast to verse 1. Whereas he was

33

thirsty and hungry, here he is full and fat. Notice the metaphors of lips and mouth that pervade this psalm (vv. 3, 5, 11). The word "soul" also ties these two verses together.

Verse 6 also complements verse 1. In verse 1 the speaker seeks God in the morning. In verse 6 he remembers Him in bed and thinks about Him during the night watches. In verse 1 he was in a land parched by the sun; in verse 7 he enjoys the shade under God's wings.

An interesting contrast is found in verse 8. The psalmist cleaves to God and God holds him. There is something in this verse for both positions on the question of the security of the believer. From a human viewpoint we must stick fast to Him, but from God's perspective He holds us in His right hand, the position of favor.

Verse 9 begins the little maledictory section of the psalm. The Hebrew grammar allows the word "destroy" to go with "my soul" or "life," as it is in the standard translations, or to describe the enemies. The latter option would read: "They will be for destruction who seek my soul/life." If this is correct then there are four curses in verses 9 and 10: destruction, dispatch to the underworld, sword, and jackals or foxes.

Another promise concludes the psalm (v. 11). Speaking in the third person, the king sees the day when he and all who live in God will rejoice and glory, while all the mouths of the liars will be shut.

# PSALM 64

Psalm 64 easily falls into a chiastic outline.

A  Prayer for deliverance from wicked *workers* (vv. 1-2)
  B  Description of the wicked *tongue* (v. 3)
    C  Purpose of the wicked *shooting* (v. 4)
      D  Psychology of the wicked (vv. 5-6)
    C  God *shoots* the wicked (v. 7)
  B  God confounds their *tongue* (v. 8)
A  Righteous men enjoy the *work* of God (vv. 9-10)

The italicized words indicate the various paired elements. These are not merely coincidental English translations but represent paired Hebrew words as well. In addition, the word "suddenly" occurs in verses 4 and 7, and "arrows" in verses 3 and 7.

The turning point in the psalm is after verse 6. Up to that point it is a prayer and complaint about secret enemies. From verse 7 on is the anticipating of their condemnation and the vindication of the righteous.

The psalm begins with three words of entreaty: Hear me, preserve me, and hide me. Verses 1-2 are only loosely parallel within themselves. The "fear of the enemy" (v. 1) deserves some comment. Sometimes fear of something or someone can be as destructive as the harm itself. Fear can sap our ability to concentrate, can challenge our faith, and virtually destroy our usefulness. Living under the threat of danger can be more disastrous than the catastrophe itself. Knowing something of this, the psalmist prays for deliverance from such fear. This is a different word from the one rendered "fear" in verses 4 and 9.

The general introduction to the description of tne enemy

begins with their appellations: wicked plotters and workers of iniquity (v. 2). On the one hand is the private planning session where the wicked plot to overthrow the righteous; then there is the overt execution of that plan, the insurrection (KJV), the tumult (ASV), or the turbulent mob (NEB*).

As in other psalms, the focus is first on what the wicked say and then on what they do. So verses 3 and 4 speak of their tongue as a sword and their words as arrows. The adjective "bitter" may mean "poisonous," but the antiquity of poisonous arrows has not been established. Like any assassin, they seek to make the kill privately and at a time when the victim's guard is down, hence suddenly. The word "fear" is the same word as in verse 9 and contains the ideas of reverence, honor, and respect, as well as awesome fear. Naturally, they do not honor their victim.

Verses 5 and 6 are a reconstruction of what goes through the minds of wicked men. The dastardly plot is a corporate venture. They convince themselves that their crime will go undetected and unpunished, a gamble which every criminal takes. In the latter half of verse 6, the Hebrew text has only four words: *and near, a man, and a heart,* and *deep.* Undoubtedly they reflect the context which has to do with secret plotting. Most translations emend the Hebrew text or add words in order to produce a meaningful line.

The *but* at the beginning of verse 7 shows the other side of the coin. They shoot at God's man; now God will shoot back. They plan a sudden attack; God will suddenly wound them. They whet their tongue as a sword; God will make them fall by their own tongue.

Three groups of people react three ways to this phenom-

*The New English Bible with Apocrypha* (New York: Oxford University Press and Cambridge University Press, 1970).

enon. God has made their plans backfire, and He has answered prayer and delivered the psalmist. First, all who witness it will run. Second, all men will think and declare God's work with reverent fear. Third, the righteous, those delivered, will rejoice and glory in the refuge that the Lord provides.

When God occasionally chooses to do something extraordinary, and obvious to all men, people react differently. Some ignore it, or run, or wag their heads. Others recognize and perhaps wisely consider it. But only the believers, the upright in heart, rejoice. In which group are you?

## PSALM 65

Psalm 65 is a praise psalm which is optimistic, refreshing, positive, and wholesome. No enemies are cursed. No imprecations are prayed down on anyone. No complaints are registered. The first half focuses on God's greatness, while the latter half has an agricultural setting and obviously reflects the happiness that a good harvest brings. Some suggest, and it is grammatically possible, that verse 9 begins a prayer for rain. That explanation is not necessarily better or improved.

No outline is discernible in the psalm. Rather, the movement from idea to idea is somewhat like prose. Verses 1-2 are like an invocation. The first line has an interesting expression; the word "wait" is the word "silent," hence, wait in silence. Perhaps the praise is silent until the vows and petitions are made.

Just as our prayers ought to contain an element of confession and a plea for forgiveness, so verse 3 does that in this psalm. "Forgive" here is the word "atone" or "cover," used of the cover of the Ark of the Covenant, the Mercy Seat.

37

Another great theological truth, election, is in verse 4. The verse appears to state exactly what Jesus said in John 6:44 (NIV*): "No one can come to me, unless the Father who sent me draws him." From the "he" in the first half of verse 4 the psalmist changes to "we," implying that he is among those chosen. These references to the Temple may show that the psalm is later than David, who did not live to see the Temple which his son Solomon built. Neither the authority of the titles nor the exclusive use of this term for Solomon's Temple is a conclusive argument for dating this psalm.

Just as the words "fear" and "awful" in the Bible need reinterpretation, so does "terrible" (v. 5). It is built on the root word for "holy fear" or simply points to those acts of God which prompt our awe and reverence. Because of the reference to the ends of the earth, verse 5 may be Messianic or eschatological. Most occurrences of this kind are definitely futuristic. It is altogether possible that the more enlightened psalmist envisioned the day when God's Kingdom would have worldwide subjects. From the Jerusalem point of view the Western Hemisphere would be at the end of the world.

Continuing the praise of God's cosmic deeds, verses 6 and 7 speak of His establishing the mountains and stilling the oceans as well as the people.

Verse 8 easily picks up the thought of the closing line of verse 7, but also echoes verse 5. People in faraway places will react to the evidence that God exists. This natural revelation is apparent morning and evening.

Beginning with verse 9, the focus of the psalm is on God's blessing in the realm of agriculture. A series of nine benign

*The New International Version of the New Testament (Grand Rapids: Zondervan, 1973).

actions carry on through verse 11. From the general statement at the head of the list, "You visit the earth," a progression is evident. God waters, enriches, provides, irrigates, and so forth. The culmination comes when He crowns the year with goodness and, in highly figurative language, makes "thy paths drip with fatness" (NASB). Up and down the paths are vegetables and fruits which have spilled off the overloaded wagons.

The exalted speech carries on to the end of the poem. Hills are wrapped in joy. Pastures are clothed with flocks. Valleys are so covered with grain that the actual ground is hidden. The paths, pastures, hills and valleys all shout and sing. It is a picture of abundance but also one of answered prayer and vows performed. Such a small price for such a cornucopia of blessing!

## PSALM 66

All the psalms from 51 to 65 have David's name in the title. But just as that may not necessarily mean authorship, so the absence of his name in Psalm 66 may not necessarily mean he was not the author.

Like Psalm 65, Psalm 66 is a praise psalm. We are urged to give glory to the One who has created the world and redeemed His people. Up through verse 12 the terms are you, we, our, and us, while in verses 13-20 the first personal pronouns predominate: I, my, and me. Again, due to the generalities in the psalm, it is impossible to pinpoint the time and place of composition.

A number of imperatives mark the psalm, beginning with, "Make a joyful noise" (v. 1) to, "Come and hear" (v. 16).

The opening verses are cosmic and universal. "All the earth" (v. 4) is summoned to praise. Compare verses 1 and 4. Only later in the psalm is God's greatness narrowed to the deliverance of the children of Israel from Egypt (v. 6) and finally to what God did for the psalmist personally (v. 16).

Verses 1-4 overflow with terms for praise: joyful noise, glory, his name, terrible (awesome, NASB), greatness, power, worship, and sing. Several words occur more than once as if to show that the language has been exhausted in his effort to adequately praise God. A somewhat explainable "selah" closes this section.

Beginning with verse 5 the psalmist demonstrates the awe-inspiring works of God first mentioned in verse 3. Verse 6 definitely refers to the Exodus from Egypt. The record of the sea turning to dry land is in Exodus 14:21; the crossing of the Jordan River on foot is in Joshua 3:16. Recounting the events of the Exodus is a common motif in the Bible. Moses did it over and over in Deuteronomy (cf. Deu 5:15). Psalm 106:9 is just one of many examples of it in the Psalter. And New Testament preachers such as Stephen likewise referred to the Exodus, that archetype of deliverance (Ac 7:36).

Verse 7 is more general but may apply to the events connected with the takeover of the promised land. A second "selah" precedes verse 8 which is a charge to bless God. That benediction introduces a somewhat negative introspection which runs to verse 12. Although the beginning of the series (v. 9) and the end (v. 12c) are positive, verses 10-12b are almost a complaint. The total impact is that God has been faithful through thick and thin, through many trials and troubles. Those adversities constitute the middle part of this four-verse section. God refined them like precious metal. Job testified to the same ordeal in Job 23:10. If we translate the verb in verse 10 as "assay" the idea of metal-testing comes across better.

The next trial was to be trapped like an animal in a net. The third (v. 11*b*) was hard work, perhaps slavery. The fourth was war (v. 12*a*), and then the natural catastrophes of fire and flood (cf. Is 43:2).

Finally, and with the important disjunctive conjunction "but" (v. 12), the psalmist declares that God brought us into an abundant place. That inherited wealth prompts generosity in return, as the next verses (13-15) record vows of service and sacrifice.

The psalm has turned more personal in verse 13, but there is no reason to see a new poet or even a major break in the thought. Think about verse 14. How many people make vows when they are in distress, and extravagant promises to God in times of crises, and forget them when life is calm once more! Not so this ancient saint. He looked for the day when prosperity would again be his lot, when his personal storm would be over, and immediately set his accounts right with God. Somehow we think that because we cannot see God, He cannot see us and therefore He will not remember or demand our promissory notes.

A third "selah" introduces the concluding call to praise and testify of received grace. The "come and hear" (v. 16) is similar to the "come and see" (v. 5). The psalmist briefly reiterates in general terms that God has answered prayer. A little lesson on the necessity of confession of sin constitutes verse 18. The older word "regard" isn't as good as the simple Hebrew word meaning "see." This note needs to be re-sounded since so many public and, presumably, private prayers neglect confession. In fact, this may be the major reason for unanswered prayer. God will forgive sin only when it is confessed.

Apparently there was no known or unconfessed sin in this godly poet. God did hear his prayer. Therefore he utters his concluding *baruch,* "blessed be God," whose steadfast covenant love never fails.

## PSALM 67

A simple chiasmus forms the structure of Psalm 67:

A  God will bless us (v. 1)
   B  God's way on earth (v. 2)
      C  Let the peoples praise you (v. 3)
         D  Nations joy in God's judgment (v. 4)
      C  Let the peoples praise you (v. 5)
   B  Earth yields produce (v. 6)
A  God will bless us (v. 7)

Verses 3 and 5 are absolutely identical. Verses 1 and 7 have identical forms of the verb "bless," though in English they are translated differently. The word "earth" connects verses 2 and 6, while the middle verse (4) has internal similarities.

Most scholars conclude that this is a harvest song with the Feast of Tabernacles as the appropriate occasion. In particular, verse 6 gives this lead. The verbs of verse 1 can be rendered as prayers, as they are in the King James Version (grammatically speaking, as *jussives*), or as simple futures as in verse 7. Because they can express a wish, some Bible students understand the psalm as a prayer for rain, though that is never expressly stated. The Aaronic benediction of Numbers 6:24-26 is quite similar to verse 1.

In both verses 2 and 7 there are expressions which speak of the whole world. Usually such terms as "all nations" or "ends of the earth" are Messianic and eschatological, or at least missionary. From the earliest times God had a plan to include in His Kingdom subjects from all over the world. The universal nature of the Church was not a new idea nor a parenthetical measure in the plan of the ages. Throughout the Psalms and very specifically in such places as Isaiah 49: 6, the worldwide spread of the Gospel is anticipated.

Applying verses 1 and 2 to the present, God is merciful and blesses us in order that we might make known His ways in the world and His salvation to all nations. Verse 3 is the result of the conversions of all the people. Let these newly regenerated ones join the chorus of praise. This refrain comes again in verse 5.

The central verse of the psalm (v. 4), ties in very neatly with the preceding and succeeding verses. The "nations" are not only parallel to the "peoples" in verses 3 and 5, but the same nations to whom God's salvation was made known in verse 2 are here praising Him. The word "earth" occurs in verse 4 as well as in verses 2, 6, and 7. These nations are happy to have God as their Judge, not in the sense of Condemner but in the sense of Leader and Vindicator, Sovereign and Justifier.

Verse 6 is the only specific reference to harvest, but since the terminology of the rest of the psalm is so vague, this serves well to reflect the occasion of the psalm. The benediction which closes the song begins in verse 6b, but verse 7 summarizes the two major thrusts. God will bless us. He will be worshiped everywhere.

The questions left to us are: What are we doing with His blessings? Are we keeping them to ourselves? Are we offering only private praise? Or are we telling the world about Jesus? Are we letting the ends of the earth know about the wonderful ways of God, His blessed plan of salvation?

43

# PSALM 68

Psalm 68 is among the most difficult to translate. It has thirteen words in it which occur nowhere else in the Hebrew Bible. It is difficult to date. Guesses range from a very ancient but updated ode to the time of the Maccabees. It is difficult to classify. Almost every kind of literature is found here: praise, thanksgiving, historical reminiscence, complaint, imprecation, and prayer.

The psalm is most like Judges 5 in its style. Basically, it praises God for past victories. Many of the suggestions center around the Ark of the Covenant and its being brought to Jerusalem (2 Sa 6), or taken into battle against the Ammonites (2 Sa 11:11). These suggestions are in spite of the Ark not being mentioned specifically in the psalm. Either of these occasions comports, however, with the title which attributes the song to David.

Some Bible students see here a veiled history of Israel beginning with the Exodus (v. 7) and continuing through the Millennium (v. 31), including such events as the death of Ahab (v. 23) and the Passover of Hezekiah (v. 27). Others take the events before David as historical allusions and the later events as predictions in order to avoid a later dating and preserve the Davidic authorship.

Probably more technical articles are available on this enigmatic psalm than any other. Without pursuing the questions of date, authorship, occasion, and classification any further, turn to the text itself. Verses 1-2, apart from the opening line, are curses on the enemy in general. The psalmist prays that their disarray and dissolution will be like vanishing smoke or melting wax. The prayer for the righteous (v. 3), on the other hand, is for their happiness and rejoicing before God.

44

From the wish form of the verb in verses 1-3 the author turns to imperatives in verse 4, the only such imperatives until verse 28. The words "extol" (KJV), or "cast up a highway" (ASV), or "lift up a song" (RSV) use the Hebrew root *salal,* about the only lexicographical cognate for the mysterious "selah" (cf. remarks on Ps 3).

Many different names for God occur in this psalm. In verse 4c is "YAH," a shortened form of the holy, unpronounced four letters *YHWH.* The full name is in verse 16. "Lord" (*Adonai*) occurs six times. "The God" (*Ha'el*) appears twice. "The Almighty" (*Shaddai*) is in verse 14, and the combinations "GOD the Lord" and "YAH" or "LORD God" are found in verses 20 and 18, respectively. God is called "King" in verse 24. The most common name, simply "God" (*Elohim*), is used twenty-five times in the Hebrew in these thirty-five verses.

An exalted recitation of God's mighty and merciful deeds begins in verse 5 and continues off and on to the end of the work. Verses 5-6 praise God for His greatness and compassionate concern for lonely orphans, widows, and prisoners.

Verses 7-18 echo various triumphs connected with the Exodus from Egypt and the conquest of Canaan. This is very clear from verses 7 and 8, but not so evident from other verses. Psalm 78 (vv. 12 ff.) is much more explicit in its review of this great deliverance.

An example of the elliptical form of the poetry in this psalm is in verse 8. It presents a variety of the staircase or progressive parallelism. Read it without the added words:

The earth trembled;
The heavens dropped at God's presence;
This Sinai            at God's presence, the God of Israel.

No one questions the connection of this verse to Exodus 19: 18.

The "rain" (v. 9) cannot be found in the accounts of the wilderness wanderings, although the word "dropped" (v. 8) may refer to the manna as it does in Psalm 78:24. Because the Hebrew word for "publishers" in verse 11 is feminine, some see the army of publishers of God's news as women (ASV, NASB). Hence the allusions to Miriam (Ex 15:20), Deborah (Judg 5:1), or the women who sang at David's victorious return from the Philistines (1 Sa 18:6). Furthermore, verse 12 may allude to Sisera and Jael (Judg 4:17 ff.), even as the expression in verse 13 sounds like Judges 5:16a. The Hebrew words are nearly identical in these two passages.

Verse 13 introduces the most difficult part of the psalm. The Revised Standard Version has produced sense by connecting the women at home in verse 12 with those among the sheepfolds ("pots," KJV) in verse 13; and the spoil (v. 12) with the silver and gold of verse 13. Verse 14 continues to spell out the means God used to rout Israel's enemy. The only other mention of Zalmon (v. 14, RSV) in Scripture is Judges 9:48, but it contains no mention of snow. The King James Version translators chose to insert the word "white," thinking that the connection between the scattered kings and the snow was the color. The American Standard Version, Revised Standard Version, Berkeley, and New English Bible make the analogy on the scattering itself. The Jerusalem Bible* juggles the verses around, likening the snow to the glittering spoil.

From verses 15 and 16 comes the idea of the Ark of the Covenant going up to Jerusalem. Because God has chosen to abide in Zion, the other mountains, particularly in Bashan in northern Trans-Jordan, are envious.

*The Jerusalem Bible (Garden City, N.Y.: Doubleday, 1966).

Chariots are ordinarily connected with war and may reflect the Ark going into battle (v. 17). We know that such a practice was common (1 Sa 4:3). Perhaps "Sinai" is elliptical for "the God of Sinai."

Paul's quotation of verse 18 in Ephesians 4:8 has made it famous. Here it refers to God ascending a mountain, leading away rebellious captives, and accepting the spoils of war. The scene changes in verse 19, which opens with "Blessed be the Lord." The very familiar but italicized words of the King James Version, of course, are not in the original. The meaning might well be that God carries us or our burdens. That He should load us or oppress us is inconsistent with the context. These two verses (19-20) are definitely praise.

Whereas the preceding verses are benediction, verses 20-23 are imprecation. The language is very gory but not unlike the way wars were fought. Because dogs like the enemy's blood (v. 23) and they are referred to in an incident involving King Ahab (1 Ki 22:38), some make that a definite connection. This is not necessary. It merely points to the ignominious death of the foe, and similar occurrences probably took place at every battle.

The setting is more beatific beginning with verse 24. God, perhaps meaning the Ark of the Covenant, enters the sanctuary in the midst of singing and dancing. Verse 27 notes that one of the smallest, one of the largest, and two of the most distant tribes join in the celebration.

Verses 28-35 are more eschatological than historical. If the psalm is Davidic, then the "temple" (v. 29) was not in existence yet. That and the universal response to God's rule point to a future day. Note that kings bring presents (v. 29), that princes from Egypt and Ethiopia come to worship God (v. 31; cf. Is 18:7; 45:14), and that the kingdoms of the earth are urged to sing praise to the Lord (v. 32). The language of verses 30 and 33 also is exalted. Verse 30 beseeches God to rebuke the foreign leaders, pictured here as bulls. Parts of this verse reflect terms in verses 13-14. Several expressions also found in the Ugaritic literature appear in this psalm. One describes the Deity as "him who rides in the heavens" (v. 33 [RSV]; cf. v. 4; Is 19:1).

The praise section continues to the end of the psalm and the kingdoms are urged to ascribe strength to God (v. 34). Next follow three statements regarding God's strength and excellency. As if in a fanfare of praise, the climax is reached as the people confess that the blessed God gives them strength and power.

Though the language is difficult and the thread of logic impossible to follow through this poem, nevertheless it teaches something to the diligent reader. It shows that God can be seen and given glory for His innumerable deeds, great and small. It teaches that any praise or successes we have come from Him and therefore we should give back praise to Him. The very exalted nature of this work points up that we do not yet know everything about the Hebrew language, the culture, or the modes of praise. Let us simply respond with intelligence, humility, sobriety, and reverence to what we do know of them. Blessed be God.


## PSALM 69


Psalm 69 is an individual lament. Because several New Testament writers apply verses in it to Christ, the psalm is also Messianic. Apart from the lament portions, the psalm includes prayers for deliverance, and imprecations. In fact, the opening line is a prayer, but it is followed immediately by complaints.

Verses 1*b*-2 picture the psalmist's distress as an overflowing flood. Knowing how little the ancient Israelites had to do with the sea, and that there are no records of their ever swimming, the thought of drowning must have been real indeed. The expression in verse 1 about the water coming to the soul may refer to near drowning, since the word for soul is connected with breath. Some modern translators use the word "neck" (RSV; NEB). No one takes the picture of the flood literally. Rather, the flood of troubles or enemies is clearly in view for the rest of the psalm. These figures appear in the prayer of verses 14 and 15.

The picture changes in verse 3 to that of a man with dried-out throat and failing eyes. Perhaps the throat is dry from calling for help and the eyes weary with weeping. Having described himself and his condition, the writer turns in verse 4 to his numerous enemies. With some hyperbole he charges that they that hate him are more than the hairs of his head. Jesus cited this verse in reference to Himself in John 15:25. The charge against the innocent is that he must pay back what he has not taken. This is just the opposite of redemption, which means to purchase back what belongs to you.

In verse 5 the complaint turns to prayer. First comes the confession and protestation of innocence, followed in verse 6 by requests for exoneration for the good people. The two occurrences of "for my sake" are very interesting. If these do refer to Christ then this is His prayer: that we should enjoy boldness and honor.

What the righteous sufferer endured was a result of his obedience and zeal. If he had not been God's man he would not have reaped the unpopularity he did. Verse 8 may have been in John's mind when he spoke the words recorded in

John 7:3-5, that even Jesus' brothers did not believe on Him. John 2:17 unquestionably refers to Psalm 69:9. The zeal that Jesus showed when He ran the merchandisers out of the Temple was a zeal, a jealousy, for God's house. The Temple must be, He was saying, a place of prayer. If the world hates God and His Son then the Christian can expect to be hated too. For, in the terminology of verse 9, those who reproach God will reproach His followers. In Romans 15:3 Paul applies this last half verse to Christians.

The next three verses (10-12) are not specifically mentioned in the New Testament but certainly do depict a righteous man being mocked for his piety. Certain phrases in Job correspond with this psalm. For instance, compare verse 8 with Job 19:13-15 and verse 11 with Job 17:6. Although the New Testament writers never make the connection, certain parallels between the righteous suffering of Job and Christ do exist.

The pendulum of complaint and prayer swings to supplication (v. 13). Generalities introduce the petitions and then turn specifically to a plea for deliverance (vv. 14 ff.). Some of the synonyms used for the watery plight of verses 1-2 are repeated in verses 14-15. Although the word Sheol does not appear in this psalm, some commentators believe that this psalm in general, and verse 15 in particular, is a prayer for deliverance from death. It is a moot question.

The prayer section continues through verse 29. Verses 16-18 are still on the lofty level of the devout and patient sufferer. Such choice words as "lovingkindness, tender mercies, redeem, and ransom" (ASV) occur.

In verses 19-20 the theme is one of complaint and self-pity. Instead of comforters, only reproachers can be found; instead of a sympathetic ear only a hostile adversary.

50

The focus of the charge against the enemy is in verse 21. All four of the gospel writers cite this verse as they record the events at Golgotha (Mt 27:34, 48; Mk 15:23; Lk 23:36; Jn 19:28-30). Can anyone doubt that these inspired chroniclers took Psalm 69:21 as Messianic? No records exist of David or any other Old Testament saint suffering this ignominy.

The imprecatory part of the passage encompasses verses 22-28. Several of these curses are cited in the New Testament. Verses 22-23 are used by Paul in Romans 11:9-10. Notice that Paul concurs with the psalm title and ascribes the work to David. Peter quoted verse 25 in Acts 1:20 and applied it to Judas Iscariot. Compare also Jesus' allusion to the verse (Mt 23:38; Lk 13:35), as He applied this curse to the people of Israel as a whole.

Verse 26 provides an interesting insight into the sovereignty of God. As Isaiah and others indicate (Is 53:10), the Messiah's suffering was in God's eternal plan. It was not a mistake, a miscalculation, an accident, a reversal, or a postponement of God's program. Men only crucified Him who was slain before the foundation of the world (1 Pe 1:20; Rev 13:8).

The last seven verses (30-36) move our attention from the cross to glory. None of these verses is mentioned in the New Testament, but obviously the prayers have been answered and the victory attained. First there is general praise with song and thanksgiving. Then follows the great truth of the New Testament: the sufficiency and efficacy of the substitutionary atonement of Christ. Unlike the often repeated sacrifices of oxen and bulls in the Old Testament, the once for all death of Christ made additional sacrifices and oblations cease (Heb 9:11-12; 10:9-12).

The psalm continues triumphantly to the end. The meek, the needy, and the despised are all vindicated. Not only do they praise God but also the whole creation joins in the glorious chorus. This is the fulfillment of the prediction of Romans 8:21. The now groaning creation groans because of the Fall but will, on that great day, be released from bondage and join in the song of the redeemed. Such a thought is particularly welcome at this time of ecological concern.

The restored Edenic bliss is especially illustrated by a rebuilt and repopulated Zion, enjoyed and occupied by the believers who love God's name. So a psalm that begins with a drowning man concludes with a renewed planet and a redeemed people.

## PSALM 70

Except for a few minor variations, Psalm 70 is identical to Psalm 40:13-17. By itself this psalm is a prayer for help against persecutors. A simple chiastic outline fits these five verses, for verses 1 and 5 have both similar words and sentiments. The interior verses, 2-4, have jussive (wish form) verbs. Verses 2-3 are imprecations on the enemy, while verse 4 is a prayer for God's people.

The title of the psalm has the additional Hebrew word meaning "to bring to remembrance." This may have something to do with the fact that this is a repetition of part of another psalm. There is no good reason to deny David's authorship. The first and most obvious variation from Psalm 40 is in the opening words. Psalm 40:13 has "be pleased" while Psalm 70 has nothing corresponding with that opening plea. Many translations repeat the words "make haste" from the second stich.

Verses 2-3 constitute the curse section. The psalmist puts a curse on those who would put a curse on him. Notice the use of "seek" in verses 2 and 4. The wicked seek the soul of the righteous but the righteous seek God.

The urgency of the situation is reiterated again in verse 5, the echo of verse 1. Not only is "make haste" repeated, but the concluding words are "make no tarrying," or in modern English, "Don't be late." The verb "make haste," incidentally, occurs in the name of Isaiah's son, Maher-shalal-hash-baz (quicken-loot-make haste-plunder). Oh, to find that delicate balance in our prayer life between pious urgency and patient waiting!

## PSALM 71

The clue that Psalm 71 is the prayer of an old man comes from verse 9. Since God has been with him from birth (v. 6), he trusts that He will not forsake him now (v. 18). The prayer is comprised of elements of testimony, praise, complaint, and imprecation.

Following an initial declaration of trust, the psalm opens with a series of petitions. In general terms the psalmist prays to be spared shame and invokes God to bow His ear, deliver, rescue, and save him. He calls God his Rock, an epithet used over and over by Moses in Deuteronomy 32. Two characteristics of a rock are applicable to God. First, He is the foundation. And since this word indicates mountain-size rocks, the term implies protection. Notice that Jesus is the Rock in the New Testament (1 Co 10:4; cf. Dan 2:45).

Verses 5-8 recollect the providential care God took of the psalmist from the womb (v. 6), through youth (v. 5), right up to old age (v. 9). Verse 7*a* can be taken two ways. Either in his affliction, like Job, the psalmist remained faithful and thus was a wonder, or he was always blessed and no harm ever befell him. That would also be a wonder. Nothing in the immediate context points to the first explanation, so the second seems better. Many of God's people can relate amazing deliverances and near-miraculous exploits, while unbelievers show nothing but awe and ignorant wonder. The enemy can understand neither our faith nor the mercy of our God.

Now that the years have taken their toll on the psalmist, he pleads for continued grace (v. 9). Perhaps only now his enemies are forming a coalition against him, as verse 10 indicates. Their words are quoted in verse 11 while the answer of faith is in verse 12. Notice how the foe tries to bring God into his argument and so to sanction his wickedness. Rabshakeh displayed similar arrogance when he tried to convince King Hezekiah of Judah to surrender (Is 36:10). He was not the first and he will not be the last to do evil hypocritically in the name of righteousness, to work against God while claiming cooperation with God.

The shame from which he prayed to be spared (v. 1), the psalmist now invokes on his enemies (v. 13). This is the only imprecatory verse in the psalm and it immediately yields to more pleasant, positive praise in the succeeding verses.

A difficult phrase ends verse 15. The Jerusalem Bible (fn. 71 d.) takes it to be a scribe's comment, "I have not known how to read the letters," on the following word in verse 16. More traditional renderings take it to apply to the numerous righteous acts of God or the innumerable days one will enjoy God's salvation. In this respect the phrase is like Psalm 40:5.

Verses 17-18 again quickly scan the writer's life from youth to gray hairs. He makes the point that, since God has been faithful up to the present, He will continue to bless so that a testimony of His goodness may be passed on to other generations. Verse 20 is one of those rare references in the Old Testament to the resurrection of the dead. To be sure, one might say this is merely hyperbole for temporal troubles, but since the psalmist has described his life from youth to old age, what other deliverance could he anticipate except resurrection from the dead?

The fact that the psalmist speaks of accompanying himself with two varieties of stringed instruments does not prove that he was an accomplished musician or a professional functionary at the Temple. The poet is searching for noble terms with which to exalt God. Altogether he says he will do four things: "I will praise . . . I will sing . . . I will shout . . . I will talk" (ASV). Like many "trouble and trust" psalms, this one too ends as if the prayer of the earlier parts is already answered. The psalmist declares that those who sought his hurt have been put to shame. The enemy's confounding (v. 24) may serve as a commentary on verse 7. While the righteous are redeemed and blessed, the wicked are ashamed and confounded.

## PSALM 72

The second book in the Psalter ends with Psalm 72. Only this and Psalm 127 are attributed to Solomon in the title. (KJV reads "for Solomon," while the same particle is rendered "of" when used with David.)

Many of the grandiose things said about the king in this psalm are too exalted to refer to an earthly monarch so there is a long Jewish and Christian tradition that this is a Messianic psalm. No New Testament writer, however, ever cites it or applies it to Christ. Three explanations are possible: (1) the psalm is full of hyperbole but applies only to a king such as Solomon and perhaps was written for his coronation; (2) it is Messianic, although ignored by the gospel writers and apostles; (3) it is full of double meanings and is to be read with two individuals in view, Israel's ancient king and Jesus Christ the Lord.

Most of the verbs can be read as wishes, as in the Revised Standard Version or the Anchor Bible.\* If this is so, then this psalm is primarily a prayer. If the verbs are read as simple futures, Psalm 72 is a predictive psalm. This latter form is used in the King James Version and American Standard Version. Other modern translations such as The Jerusalem Bible and the New English Bible mix the forms.

The first four verses have a strong political or judicial overtone befitting a kingly figure. Several different words for the idea of righteous justice occur here. The appellation, "king's son," in verse 1 fits with the title, since Solomon was both the king and the son of the king.

Throughout the psalm the ministry of this king includes both international functions and social concerns. This very domestic facet of his reign is introduced in verse 2 where he executes justice for the poor. "Judge," of course, does not mean, as it now generally does, "to condemn," but rather "to adjudicate" or "to administer law." Such administration may result in condemnation or vindication. In connection with the poor, it usually involves legal defense leading to protec-

\*The Anchor Bible (Garden City, N.Y.: Doubleday, 1968).

tion and exoneration. This theme reappears in verses 4, 12, 13, and 14.

Verse 3 has exalted language but may point to the idyllic situation prevalent during the reign of this earthly king. Rather than the terror which often lurks in the mountains there will be peace. Or the figure may refer symbolically to the crops that grow on mountains and hills. Rather than producing hostile and evil thorns, the harvest will be of peace and righteousness.

The eternal character of this ideal king's reign is like the enduring sun and moon (v. 5). Another illustration of his faithful and beneficent rule occurs in verse 6. Like regular and necessary rain, his benevolence will shower on his subjects.

In verses 7-8 appear some of the terminology that is too exalted for Solomon and fits better with Christ. The several references to peace (*shalom*) link the psalm with Solomon (*Shelomo*) but might also point to Christ, the Prince of Peace (*Sar Shalom*). It is simply not true that the peace of Solomon outdistanced the moon. Nor did he control the ends of the earth, or even the earth as he knew it. These things are true of Christ, however. The peace He brings endures. He already has subjects of every nation of the world. This will become undeniably evident and more completely fulfilled when He returns.

While verse 9 continues the eschatological and lofty description, verse 10 easily applies to the Solomon of the Old Testament. Second Chronicles 9:21 records the Tarshish tribute, while 1 Kings 10:1 mentions Sheba's contribution. Seba's location is more uncertain than Sheba's. Probably they are both far to the south, since Tarshish is to the north and west.

The psalmist reverts to terminology describing the world-wide reign again in verse 11. Here, too, this is being fulfilled in Christ in a way that only could apply to Solomon by using gross exaggeration.

Verses 12-14 again focus on the immediate social or domestic feature of the administration of this great but humble king. These passages echo in Isaiah 11:2-5; 42:3; 61:1-2; and elsewhere. The last line of verse 14 reminds one of Psalm 116:15, "Precious in the sight of the LORD is the death of his saints."

Just as certain verses would not fit Solomon, so the middle stich of verse 15 does not fit the Messiah. He is not prayed *for* but *to*. This is not a preposition that can mean anything else but "for" or "in behalf of." However, men did bring gold to both Solomon and Jesus (cf. Mt 2:11).

An idyllic picture of agricultural abundance and expanding population comes in verse 16. The reference to grain growing on the mountaintops may link this verse with verse 3. Referring to the last of the three promises in this verse, overpopulation was never given a thought. Large families were an economic blessing and populated cities were a military advantage. Only in recent times have too many people been a problem.

Once more (v. 17) the eternality of this king's reign is stressed. That all nations should be blessed in him definitely sounds like Genesis 12:3 and 22:18, where a similar promise was given to Abraham. An appropriate and blessed benediction concludes the psalm and this second book of the Psalter. The first line at least is like Zacharias' benediction in Luke 1:68. Interestingly, God's name occurs only in the first and last verses of this psalm. A double "Amen" brings to a close the body of the psalm.

Verse 20, appended to the psalm, indicates this to be the

end of David's prayers. Perhaps this psalm was a prayer by him for Solomon as well as for his greater Son. David's name continues to occur in psalm titles (e.g., 86, 101, 103), but perhaps they cannot be called prayers and so this postscript is correct.


## PSALM 73


The third book of the Psalter opens with a series of psalms attributed to Asaph (Ps 73-83). Perhaps he was the author. Perhaps they were written under his administration of the music program at the Jerusalem sanctuary (cf. 1 Ch 15:19 and the remarks on Ps 50). Maybe these titles only refer to a style of psalm.

Like Psalm 37, this psalm is in the wisdom category. The psalmist raises the old question: Why do the wicked prosper and the righteous suffer? In a manner similar to the preacher in Ecclesiastes he sketches a picture and produces an argument that shows the futility of being good. But verse 17 brings an abrupt change. He lifts his eyes toward God and begins to put things in the perspective of eternity. He considers the end of the wicked and reverses his opinion of the whole matter, concluding that righteousness does pay and crime does not.

The psalm begins on a note of praise but immediately changes to a note of despair and discouragement. Verse 2 anticipates the conclusion to the psalm by stating that the psalmist nearly fell for the common argument that wealth proves one's righteousness and God's blessing while sickness and poverty are evidence of evil and God's displeasure. The line of argument proceeds from verses 3-16, where this pained but imperceptive protagonist confesses that he cannot figure out life. In the course of this half of the psalm are enumerated the many benefits the wicked enjoy. First, they are prosperous (v. 3). Second, they do not suffer long and painful illness before they die. They enjoy full strength until their dying day (v. 4). Third, they have no troubles, a general term lumping all the things that make life burdensome (v. 5).

While surfeited with these temporal fortunes, the wicked continue in pride and violence. Notice the figures the poet uses to attach these attributes to the ungodly; pride is like a necklace and violence a garment. A description of their attitude continues to the summary in verse 12. With glutted appetites (v. 7) they brag of the evil and scoff at the righteous (v. 8). They shoot off their mouths toward heaven and earth (v. 9).

Interpreters differ on the meaning of verse 10. It is best to understand that the followers of the wicked stay with him and drink with him, or drink up everything he says. Their words are quoted in verse 11, and they are a blasphemous denial of God's omniscience. Little do they realize what this psalmist is later to realize: that God is aware of their sins and will ultimately judge them. Verse 12 sums up the superficial assessment of the wicked. Not only are they evil, but also while they loaf they still get rich. Psalm 37 spoke to this attitude much earlier with its opening words: "Don't fret over evildoers."

Beginning with verse 13, the psalmist focuses on the futility of good behavior. He says what we might often think: that it is of no use to have a clean heart and washed hands. He sees no immediate benefit to obedience. In fact, he suffers the opposite; daily plagues and chastening (v. 14).

The light begins to dawn (v. 15) when the righteous sage

realizes that he has an obligation to his children. He would be untrue to that trust if he let this psalm end here. Surely he could not recommend to his sons a God who is not basically just or who does not know all things. Surely he could not suggest wickedness as a way of life. Certainly what he has said in the verses above is incomplete. The coin must have another side; there must be a different perspective on life. Perhaps a visit to the sanctuary will provide the missing insight into this painful problem.

So in verse 17 the whole psalm changes character and the true wisdom nature of this poem becomes evident. From God's point of view the wicked men look different, dramatically different, diametrically opposite, in fact. Their latter end, eternity, and other weighty spiritual considerations produce a different assessment.

Whereas this ancient saint had almost slipped into the trap of wickedness (v. 2), he now realizes that it is the wicked who stand on slippery ground. And so through verse 20 the imminent and sudden overthrow of the wicked is described. "In a moment . . . utterly . . . like a dream when one awakes . . ." (NASB, RSV) and all the phantasies are gone, so will their fortunes evaporate.

Verses 21-22 record the bitter self-castigation of the psalmist. He confesses his ignorance and shortsightedness, his carnality and faithlessness. From these expressions of regret-filled unworthiness he turns to sound faith and confidence, through to the end of the psalm. He even confesses his hope to see God (v. 24), an end quite different from that of the wicked man. Verse 25 is a favorite of many of God's people and in times of crisis or discouragement can be the balm it was to this pensive poet.

Only verse 27 interrupts the felicitous picture in this half of the psalm. There, as in many other psalms, note is made

61

of the accomplished judgment of the wicked. But rather than close on such a negative observation, verse 28 once more underscores the essential good that comes from casting one's lot with God, making Him a refuge, and putting faith in the Lord Yahweh.

## PSALM 74

Psalm 74 is a community lament. Most commentators agree that the occasion was the destruction of the Temple by the forces of Nebuchadnezzar in 586 B.C. He, then, is the madman of verse 22 (foolish man, KJV). The translation "synagogues" (v. 8) in some of the older versions has misled readers of the English Bible. The same Hebrew word is rendered "congregation" ("assembly," ASV) in verse 4. Most scholars agree that the synagogue had not begun before the exile. Others view the day of composition as later than the exile. Verse 9 is the primary clue: "There is no more any prophet." Actually, Haggai and Zechariah preached to the returned exiles.

Several rhetorical questions mark this as a lament. Notice the "why" (vv. 1, 11) and "how long" (vv. 9-10). Compare Psalms 10:1; 22:1; 44:23-24; 79:10; 80:12; and 88:14 for the former expression, and Psalms 80:4; 90:13; and 94:3 for the latter.

This psalm begins on a most discouraging note. Verses 2-3 are a prayer asking God to take note of the destruction of His people and His holy city Zion. Notice there is no repentance here. On the one hand, the psalmist appeals to God's redemption and election of Israel; on the other hand, to what the enemy has done to the sanctuary. The expression at the beginning of verse 3 means to make one's way or to pick one's steps, as the disheveled ruins would necessitate.

From verses 4-8 the psalmist elaborates on the last half of verse 3 (ASV): "all the evil that the enemy hath done." The record of Nebuchadnezzar's destruction is in 2 Kings 25:8-21, but this account is more explicit. The first offensive move was to violate the Temple's precincts, an area where no Gentiles had ever come. Verses 5-6 relate how the enemy destroyed the woodwork with axes and hatchets. After reducing the edifices to kindling, they set them on fire, along with all the other places of worship in the land (vv. 7-8).

As verse 1 of this section contained two questions, so the close has three questions (vv. 10-11).

Verses 12-17 contain praise to God for His power displayed in nature. The language is very exalted, cosmic, even apocalyptic. After a general introductory statement (v. 12) His victory over the sea creatures is stated. Some students of Ancient Near Eastern culture see here the Lord's superiority over pagan gods personified as the sea, the dragons, and the mysterious leviathan. Whether that is convincing, these verses point out God's dominion and power.

Verse 15 may allude to the Red Sea and Jordan River crossings (Jos 2:10; 3:13), or perhaps to Moses when he struck the water-laden rock (Ex 17:5-6). The events of verses 16-17 predate even the Exodus, and the creation seems to be in view (Gen 1:14-18).

Having reminded God—not that He needed reminding—of former demonstrations of power and redemptive exploits, the psalmist returns to the problem at hand. He commences with a prayer for deliverance (v. 18). His first point is the blasphemy of insulting pagans. His second point is the frailty and helplessness of the defeated Israelites (v. 19). His third point is the covenant (v. 20). Since God promises, He must fulfill. Since He vowed, He must make good. At least on this occasion the psalmist viewed the covenant as unconditional.

The prayer continues to the end of the psalm with rephrasings of the points already made. Verse 21 is like verse 19 in that it speaks of the oppression of the people of God. This ancient intercessor employs the classic for-Your-name's-sake argument in the latter half of verse 21. He implies that if God does not save His people, His honor will be clouded. Although God ultimately will answer the prayer, it is probably not for this reason.

The last two verses (22-23) are like verse 18, reiterating the charges against the heathen conqueror. The psalmist is saying, in effect: "God, answer those blasphemous fools! Don't let them have the last word! Speak for Yourself!"

On these rather bitter notes the psalm ends. To this day God's people pray that God will stem the volley of reproach that rises continually from a world of war and woe.


## PSALM 75


Because of its first verse and last two verses (9-10), Psalm 75 is in the category of praise or thanksgiving psalms. However, the central part speaks of God's judgment of the wicked, and some of those verses are in the first person. Hence, verses 2-6 are like an oracle delivered by a priest or prophet. It is impossible to set the occasion for this psalm's composition. The title is similar to that of Psalms 57-59 but attributed to Asaph rather than to David. The Hebrew words in the title or their translation, "destroy not," probably indicate a well-known tune. In no way does it agree with the contents, which are somewhat maledictory.

Verse 1 is introductory and, although the general point is obvious, the wording is open to several possibilities. No unnecessary words, in fact only eight Hebrew words, are used. Three times that many are used to convey the same meaning in the King James Version, for instance. The simplest, most word-for-word translation is as good as any others:

> We are thankful to you;
>   God, we are thankful.
> Your name is near,
>   Your wonders declare.

Remembering that "name" is tantamount to "person," the third line is readily understandable and fits nicely with the fourth. Proof of God's presence in the universe is His working of wonders.

The oracle or first-person section runs from verses 2-4, but includes the words of verses 5-6. With verse 7 God is spoken of in the third person again. The thrust of the oracle is that God is the Judge who rebukes the proud. Different translations of verse 2 are easily available. With verse 3 it serves to introduce the rebuke of verses 4-6. The psalmist sketches a quick picture of God's power. He is the One who dissolves or shakes the earth and also the One who stabilizes its pillars. A somewhat appropriate "selah" closes this scene.

The quotation continues with an attack on the arrogant or foolish (v. 4). The command not to lift up the horn is interesting. That term appears four times in this short psalm. Here as elsewhere it is a symbol of strength or pride. Compare its use (Deu 33:17; 1 Ki 22:11; Amos 6:13; Zec 1:18-21). Lifting the horns and speaking with a stiff neck are in parallel in verse 5 and not without reason, since for the

65

horns to be lifted up the neck must be stiff. This is an un-usual unmixed metaphor.

As verse 4 was cosmic in its scope so verse 6 encompasses all the world. The part about lifting up is difficult to connect with the rest of the verses and, again, many variant transla-tions are available. The translation of the Jerusalem Bible may correctly fill in this elliptical verse. It reads: "Not from the east, nor from the west, not from the desert, nor from the mountains." This is not a complete sentence and may there-fore be the introduction of verse 7 or the conclusion of verse 5.

God is Judge everywhere, putting down and setting up, to use the phrases of verse 7. Undoubtedly the psalmist uses the words "lift up" here and in verses 4, 5, and 10 (ASV) intentionally. First there is the command to the boastful not to lift up their horn; then the statement that God is the ulti-mate "lifter up" or "putter down." At the end of the psalm the prediction or testimony comes that God lifts up the horns of the righteous.

The figure of the cup of judgment fills verse 8. This theme of drinking God's wrath appears elsewhere in the Bible (cf. Job 21:20; Is 51:17; Jer 25:15; Hab 2:16). The symbol is particularly meaningful since Jesus used it when He spoke of taking the sins of the world on Himself (Mt 20:22; 26:39; Jn 18:11).

The psalmist concludes his composition with words of praise (vv. 9-10). So the psalm ends as it began, with praise. Then the figure of the horn is taken from verses 4-5 and used to sum up judgment. Psalm 1 closed in a similar manner with judgment for the wicked and vindication for the righteous.

# PSALM 76

A singer in Israel uses Psalm 76 to vocalize God's greatness, especially in the light of a particular victory. Of course the author cannot be the Asaph of 1 Chronicles 15:19 if the jubilation here is over the defeat of Sennacherib's army in 701 B.C. Perhaps it is Asaph's family or school or style. The Greek translation of the Old Testament adds the words "regarding the Assyrian" to the title. If there is truth to that addition then the possibility of the psalm pointing to that occasion in the life of King Hezekiah is all the more likely.

Both 2 Kings 18:13—19:37 and Isaiah 36-37 record the attack on Judah by the Assyrian king, Sennacherib. That threat to Jerusalem ended when the angel of the Lord struck down 185,000 enemy soldiers in one night and Sennacherib retreated to his capital in Nineveh on the upper Euphrates. The last verse of both historical accounts records the assassination of the king by his sons during his devotions in the house of his pagan god, Nisroch.

Archaeologists have uncovered verification of this biblical account. Though the famous Prisms of Sennacherib on display in Chicago and London (both originals by Sennacherib) report the siege of Jerusalem, they carefully avoid claiming destruction of the holy city or the surrender of its king. The mysterious death of the Assyrian king is alluded to in the Rassam Cylinder where Ashurbanipal tells how he punished the murderers of his grandfather, Sennacherib. The ancient historian Eusebius concurs with the Bible's account of the assassination.

With this background the psalm is more meaningful. Four different terms for the Holy Land and the holy city appear in verses 1-2. Note the parallels. "Salem" is a shortened form of Jerusalem (cf. Gen 14:18. The first part of the city name simply means "city" while "salem" means "peace.") These two unusual names (Zion and Salem) for the capital city may have been chosen to point up its holiness, antiquity, spirituality, and significance. This is not an ordinary city, not merely the seat of government, but the very place and the only place on earth where God chose to have His name dwell. "Tabernacle," as noted earlier, indicates temporal quartering. "Booths," to give another translation, were shacklike structures hastily put together in the field at harvest time to protect the workers in the heat of the day. The word for "dwelling place" is used elsewhere of the lion's den or lair. The choice of this word may point to the lionlike protection God will give His favorite city.

Verse 3 is a minimal poetic report of what God did. The language is elliptical, and the phraseology may differ from translation to translation, but the sense is apparent. God destroyed the weapons of war employed against His people. A "selah" ends this first of four three-verse stanzas. Notice that each of the four stanzas begins with a note of praise and ends with some specific feature of deliverance. Hence verses 1, 4, 7, and 10 are similar. Another "selah" would be appropriate after verse 6, according to this outline.

The figure of mountains of prey is difficult to interpret unless it is a reference to the amount of equipment abandoned by the fleeing army of Sennacherib (cf. 2 Ki 19:35-36). This interpretation is supported by what follows in verse 4.

The continuing account of the enemy sleeping (v. 5b) comports with the accounts in 2 Kings and Isaiah that the Lord's angel struck down the enemy at night. Most of them never woke up from the sleep of death that fateful night. Verse 6 elaborates on verse 5 by stating that even the chariots (or perhaps the riders) and horses were cast into a deep sleep. This is a different word for sleep than used above and indicates a torpor or sleep from which it is difficult or impossible to wake.

The third stanza (vv. 7-9) lacks the particulars in the first two stanzas. Rather, the focus is on the awe-inspiring God Himself. In view of the unusual defeat and consequent withdrawal of the surviving enemy, God is to be feared. The question involving who may "stand" in verse 7 may hark back to the incident when all the enemy were sleeping, not standing.

This deliverance of God's people was not merely a natural catastrophe or a military coincidence. It was planned by God and the sentence was issued from heaven. Neither Hezekiah nor his men had to raise a finger. They simply stood back and witnessed God's judgment on the enemy. Incidentally, Herodotus, another ancient historian, mentions Sennacherib retreating from an invasion into Egypt when field mice swept his camp and ate the strings from the bows and the straps from the shields in one night. Some connect this account with the biblical record by assuming that the rodents also carried a highly contagious and fatal plague.

Verse 10 is the best-known verse of the psalm. After one reads again the words of the arrogant and blasphemous Rabshakeh delivering the message of his equally boastful and profane king, this verse is all the more meaningful. The world would hardly know of these two men if it were not that God chose to record them in the Bible for His glory. They meant it for disgrace and shame, but God meant it for His own praise.

With verse 11 comes a command to the readers of this psalm. Having seen the justice and power of God, we are urged to bow and pay our vows to the "LORD your God." If the first half of verse 11 refers to the immediate city of Jerusalem, then the latter half refers to the surrounding country. If the first half refers to the people of Israel in particular, the latter half refers to the surrounding nations.

The last verse (12) summarizes the reasons God should be feared. He has and He will cut off the spirit of princes. That idiom might be paraphrased to say: "He brings the lies of monarchs to an end." That He did in 701 B.C., and He will do so again, for He is the terror-inspiring God.

## PSALM 77

Part of Psalm 77 reads like an individual lament, but beginning with verse 11 and especially from verse 17 on, it has the characteristics of a hymn. Notice the number of first person singular pronouns and the negative nature of the verbs in the opening verses: "I cried . . . I complained . . . I am . . . troubled." The latter part of the psalm is quite exultant and positive. The best explanation for this abrupt change is that the psalmist himself had a change of heart. Verses 11-12 hint at this. From the depths of despair he determines to count his blessings, turn his eyes on the Lord, and exercise the power of positive thinking.

In typical lamentation style the psalm opens with a groan. Although the two lines in English appear unbalanced, this is a fine example of a progressive parallel outlined as ABC, ABD. A word for word rendering would be:

> My voice to God and I cry out.
> My voice to God and he hears me.

Having stressed the intensity of the outcry, he proceeds to assert its unceasing nature. "In the day . . . in the night" are the main words of verse 2. That verse actually has four stichs, the last two connected with negative ideas. "My hand" ("sore," KJV) must be understood as the subject of the rare verb "ceased not" (KJV), or "slacked not" (ASV), or "without wearying" (RSV).

In verse 11 it is the remembering that brings this complaint to praise, but in verse 3 remembering only brings the psalmist to despair. As elsewhere, "spirit" may simply mean "breath," so here he speaks of physical as well as psychological exhaustion.

The three "selahs" in this psalm divide the poem somewhat symmetrically. One occurs at the end of verse 3. Again at the end of the complaint section there is one (v. 9). Halfway through the praise section it occurs again (v. 15). Hence the psalm is divided roughly into three parts by the "selahs," once verse 3 has been reached. (Verses 16-17 could easily have been made three verses on the basis of the number of ideas, then the division would have been even more symmetrical.)

The thought pattern does not change in verse 4, but the psalmist continues in his dejected manner, putting the blame on God. Once more he tries reflecting on the past (vv. 5-6), but such an effort only produces more despair. Unlike the therapy such introspection and recollection will produce later in the psalm, its only fruit here is the plaguing question, the problem of evil.

From time to time God's present-day children may ask the same questions as are in verses 7-9. They are not bad questions nor out of order. But they are incomplete. Never does the psalmist, and seldom does the modern saint, entertain the old-fashioned but wholesome guilt feeling. As long as God's Law shall stand and as long as man shall break it, guilt will be a part of life. Not to admit guilt is a far more

71

serious psychological and spiritual problem than suffering from too many guilt feelings.

The answer to the first five questions in verses 7-9 is "no." The answer to the last one (v. 9*b*) is "yes." It is not true that the Lord will cast off forever or that He has forgotten to be gracious. But the truth is He may be angry—angry with His people's national sins and with this psalmist's personal uncleanness.

Some scholars put this psalm in the exilic period by assuming the captivity was the supreme reason for any lament. Others, because of the archaic language, particularly of the latter part, put it in the united kingdom period or earlier.

The tune begins to change with verse 10, a verse that by itself is difficult to translate and understand. The use of italics in the older versions indicates that. Newer translations understand the Hebrew root for "years" to be the verb "change," which is altogether possible. It helps to clarify the meaning since it provides a predicate for the second half of the verse. Whatever the exact meaning of verse 10, most likely it is in agreement with the next two verses (11-12) which speak of reflecting on God's mighty deeds. Only this time such musing and recalling buoy up this sinking soul and cheer him, as well as us.

Verses 13-15 sketch God's power in general terms. He is holy. He is great. He is a Worker of wonders. He is strong. The climax and the purpose for all this power is the redemption of His people, who were the children of Jacob and Joseph in the original Exodus. After all, is not this God's great plan of the ages: to redeem a people unto Himself? All else works to this end: the creation, the Exodus, the monarchy, the offices of priest and prophets. They serve His people, prefigure Christ and His work, and blend like a symphony orchestra playing the great work of redemption.

The five concluding verses (16-20) elegantly describe the opening of the Red Sea for the children of Israel to pass through. This poet adds to the account thunder, lightning, and rain, but is certain to give God all the honor. When the waters saw God they shook. The lightning bolts are God's arrows. The thunder is His voice; the dry seabed is His path; the rescued are His people.

Altogether it is an uplifting record. It exalts God and encourages the downhearted. As spiritual physicians, let us prescribe the tonic of praise, the kind of review of God's mighty acts of redemption, such as is in verses 16-20.


## PSALM 78


The second longest in the Psalter, Psalm 78 is a didactic psalm. Verses 1-8 make the reason for this classification very plain with numerous injunctions to recite the history of Israel and to teach it to the children. The lessons of history fill the rest of the psalm to verse 72. By and large the poem is depressing, for only the bad behavior of the people is noted. The most outstanding example of disobedience is the departure of the ten northern tribes in the civil war which followed the death of Solomon in 922 B.C. (cf. Is 7:17). Verses 9-11 and 67 cite this unfortunate historical development.

This psalm is like Deuteronomy in repeating the history through the wilderness wanderings (cf. Deu 1-3). Because of this, some scholars say that Psalm 78 was used on occasions of national festivals, particularly the day of atonement. Moved to contrition by the rehearsal of the historical failures, the people would be ready to pledge renewed allegiance to the God of their fathers.

73

In verses 1-2 the psalmist writes in the first personal singular but changes to the plural in verse 3. Verse 4 states an interesting principle almost unique to Israel among ancient peoples. They made no effort to cover up the sins of their forefathers. Reconstructing the history of the countries surrounding Israel is very difficult because they rarely record some of the most significant events such as military defeats, paying of vassalage taxes, and the ignominious deaths of esteemed kings. God, in His Word, never whitewashes His heroes. All the patriarchs and prophets have their sins recorded. Perhaps God is subtly underscoring the truth that all men have sinned and come short of the glory of God, even great men such as Abraham, Moses, and David. The righteousness of God and our desperate need for Christ's atoning death stand out all the more strikingly against this black background.

Verses 7-8 sum up the introduction and the purpose for the psalm. The first reason is to evoke faith in a powerful God (v. 7). The second is to warn against backsliding and apostasy (v. 8).

Although the historical sections of the psalm (vv. 9-72) seem to stress the infidelity of Ephraim, representing the northern tribes, the story really starts with their bad attitude back in Egypt (vv. 9-12). The first marked estrangement between the north and the south is the intertribal battles recorded in Judges 20 and 21. Perhaps verse 9 refers to those days in particular.

Verse 12 begins the record of God's wonderworking against the Egyptians prior to the Exodus. Zoan, Egypt, of verse 12 still exists with the name Ṣan in the northeastern part of the Nile delta. Tanis is another name for it.

From the famous ten plagues the psalmist moves to the crossing of the Red Sea, using terminology from Exodus 15:

74

8. Then follows the record of the pillars of cloud and fire, and the miracle of water from the rock (vv. 14-16).

The account of God's faithful doings is interrupted by the account of the people's unfaithfulness (vv. 17-18). This alternation of themes persists through the psalm and points to the two lessons the children were to learn from their parents: God's love and power, and man's sin.

Next come the manna and the quails (vv. 24-30), but these too the wandering Israelites abused and so earned the displeasure of God (v. 31). Even the slaying of some Israelites failed to teach obedience to the survivors. Like the unstable waves of the sea or the constantly rising or receding tide, the devotion of the redeemed went up and down, both historically and in this song. Verse 33 marks a low point, but after judgment, their allegiance went up (vv. 34-35). However, the purity of that devotion lapsed again into deceit and falsehood (v. 36). So the history alternates between fidelity and apostasy. In between these shifting attitudes is the careful balance of the mercy and the justice of God.

By verse 43 the psalmist is repeating himself. Notice how similar the terms of verses 12 and 43 are. But in this latter section he spends more time detailing the plagues of blood, flies, frogs, and other insects and diseases. Any cross-reference Bible will lead to Moses' accounts of these momentous events.

Verse 53 (like v. 13) recounts the crossing of the sea. But in the next verses the children of Israel are already through the forty years of wilderness wandering and on the border of Canaan. Whereas the first account (vv. 11-41) quickly dispenses with the plagues and focuses on the desert rebellions, the second account (vv. 42-54) explains the plagues but hastens through the rest of the Exodus.

Beginning with verse 55, the conquest of Palestine is in

75

view with the book of Joshua as the historical backdrop. Now, rather than God providing the necessities of life—manna, water, direction—He provides victory over enemies. But again God's people are ungrateful, unfaithful, and undeserving. The arch sin of idolatry appears in verse 58. This wicked practice of the Canaanites was adopted by the people of the living, invisible God. Among the stratagems God used to bring back His people was to let the Ark of the Covenant be captured by the Philistines (v. 60). The record of this disciplinary tragedy is found in 1 Samuel 4:11.

General terms describe the havoc that prevailed as a result of God's abandoning His people (vv. 61-64). Then in due time, God went to the aid of Israel, reversed their defeats, and once more defended them against their godless enemies (vv. 65-66).

The year 922 B.C. dates the events of verses 67-68. At the death of Solomon the northern tribes abandoned their allegiance to Jerusalem and made their own independent and impious way. The psalmist describes that split in terms of God's rejecting Joseph (for his two sons, Ephraim and Manasseh, were the forebears of the larger, more influential tribes in the north) and choosing Judah, the major southern tribe, and the area where Jerusalem is located.

The record goes in reverse from verses 68-72, for verse 69 points to the building of the Temple of Solomon, which was prior to the events of verse 68. Then verse 70 backs up to the choice of David as king. And on that note exalting David, the psalm rather abruptly ends. The psalm could not have been written especially for David's coronation for, as pointed out above, it reflects very definitely the civil war of 922 B.C.

The similarity of the conclusions to Psalms 77-78 is remarkable. One ends with Moses and Aaron shepherding the flock of Israel; the other with David doing the same thing. Notice, in this final connection, the concluding verses of Psalm 79.

The lessons of Psalm 78 are as old as man. Sin has separated us from God. Though He is merciful He is also just. Though we deserve punishment, He has given grace instead. Let us not be spiritual boors like the wandering Israelites or rebellious ingrates like the tribes of Ephraim.


## PSALM 79


Psalm 79 is a national lament sprinkled with heavy doses of malediction. On the one hand, the people grieve over their defeat and on the other they pray down God's curses on the enemy. A certain ambivalence characterizes this psalm. Sometimes it reflects a noble belief in the sovereignty of God; elsewhere the logic is purely human. For instance, verse 8 makes it sound as if this defeat is part of God's purpose, His holy wrath on ancestral sins. Yet the opening verses admit no such divine direction to the recent catastrophe.

Jerusalem fell to the armies of Babylonia about 600 B.C. Against the backdrop of that dread calamity this psalm begins. The prose record of this tragedy is in 2 Kings 25:8-21, while the Book of Lamentations is entirely devoted to it.

The opening word of Psalm 79 is an invocation, a plea that God would hear this solemn complaint. The first abomination the heathen committed was to trespass into the sacred precincts of the Temple, thus profaning the earthly house of God. From that initial complaint this psalm moves on to describe the wreckage and bloodshed within the city in general. The word "heaps" at the end of verse 1 is the plural of the Hebrew *Ai,* the name of the city destroyed by Joshua after the fall of Jericho.

Among the important things in an ancient Semite's life was the hope for a decent and honorable burial. Verses 2-3 describe the indecency with which the dead of Jerusalem were treated. So here and elsewhere the ultimate ignominy, the postmortem punishment, was to be left unburied. Compare the taunt song against the king of Babylon in Isaiah 14:19, and the thrust of Psalm 53:5 and Amos 2:1.

The lament turns slightly at verse 4 and becomes more of a complaint. The psalmist is working around to the for-Your-name's-sake argument. The defeat of the holy city has brought shame directly on the people of Israel and indirectly on their God. That logic introduces the plaintive question in verse 5. These rhetorical questions are typical of the psalms of lamentation, both personal and communal (cf. Ps 13:1; 74:1; 85:5; 89:46).

With verse 6 begins the imprecatory section. Somewhere the penitent and grieving spirit of the early part of the psalm yields to bitter invective. The verbs no longer describe what has happened to God's people but command God to punish their enemies. Notice that verse 6 is the prayer and verse 7 the reason. Then verse 8*a* is another prayer and verse 8*b* the reason. Verse 6 is a prayer *against* the enemies, while verse 8 is a prayer *for* themselves.

For the sake of God's name, for His holy reputation, the psalmist prays for help, salvation, deliverance, and expiation (v. 9). The argument is expanded and explained (v. 10). Imagining what the unbelievers might say, he pleads for blood vengeance on the murderous enemy.

The imagery of verse 11 is very vivid. One can see the captured Jerusalemites languishing in a stinking Babylonian dungeon. A modern paraphrase of the last part of the verse might call these sufferers the ones on death row.

In these latter verses the pendulum swings back and forth between prayer for self and a curse on the enemy. Verse 12 is another pair of maledictions.

But the psalm ends on the more positive note of praise and testimony. Verse 13 is a promise of praise anticipating the answers to the prayers and complaints in the body of this psalm.


## PSALM 80


Addressing God as the Shepherd of Israel in verse 1 of Psalm 80 closely connects it with the preceding psalm, which ends on a similar pastoral note. This psalm, however, is more of a national prayer for restoration than a communal lament. Because Israel, Joseph, Ephraim, Benjamin, and Manasseh are mentioned in verses 1-2, the psalm probably belongs to the Northern Kingdom and may reflect its captivity in 722 B.C. Epithets for the Southern Kingdom such as Judah, Jerusalem, Zion, or David do not occur.

The superscription offers little help in determining the occasion of composition. Some Bible translations give the meaning of the Hebrew words transliterated in the older versions. *Shoshannim* means "lilies" and *Eduth* means "testimonies." The Greek translation of the Old Testament (the Septuagint) adds to the title the words, "concerning Assyria," which supports the suggestion that the psalm has to do with the fall of Samaria to the forces of Assyria (2 Ki 17: 6).

79

A refrain occurs four times with slight alteration, dividing the psalm into stanzas of unequal length. Verses 3, 7, 14, and 19 are like a chorus to the verses that precede them. The key word might be translated either "restore us" or "turn us" or "bring us back" (from captivity), except in verse 14 where a different form of the verb demands that God Himself turn. The same verbal root is the "restore" of Psalm 23:3 and the "convert" of Psalm 51:13.

The first stanza (vv. 1-2) is basically an invocation. God is urged to listen, wake up, go to work, and save His people. Among the titles given to God is "You that sit on the cherubs." This expression appears in 1 Samuel 4:4, 2 Samuel 6:2, and Psalm 99:1 and echoes Exodus 25:22, which describes the interior furnishings of the Holy of Holies.

Ephraim and Manasseh are the two sons of Joseph and the largest and most influential of the ten northern tribes. Benjamin is also important, being on the border of Judah and having within its boundaries the sanctuary city of Bethel. Remember that Joseph and Benjamin were the two favorite sons of Jacob and the only children of his first-chosen wife, Rachel.

The second stanza is more typically a lament and hence is not unlike Psalm 79. Notice the "how long" question (v. 4) and the theme of the ridiculing heathen and the damaged reputation (v. 6). The expression "angry" (v. 4) is literally "to fume" or "to smoke" (cf. Ps 74:1).

The third stanza is in parabolic form. Israel is like a vine brought out of Egypt in the Exodus and transplanted in Canaan (cf. Ho 9:10). Just as Isaiah in his fifth chapter used the same figure, so here many horticultural details appear to fill up the picture. The difference between this account and Isaiah's is that the great prophet gives the reason for the vine's rejection but the psalmist does not. Although many of the details answer to fact in the expansion of Israel, the main point is that the vine is God's, for His glory, for His use, even His to destroy. The river of verse 11 is the Euphrates, which marked the northeasternmost extremity of Israel's expansion (cf. Gen 15:18; Jos 1:4; 2 Sa 8:3; 1 Ch 5:9; 2 Ch 9:26).

The fourth stanza continues the imagery of the vine. Whereas verses 12-13 speak of the invasion of the garden by wild animals, meaning the attack of a foreign enemy, verse 16 speaks of its utter ruin by fire and pillage. Verses 14-15 go together as a prayer that continues in verse 17, except that the symbol of the vine is discontinued at that point. The psalmist continues the prayer for restoration through the end of the psalm, repeating the refrain in the last verse.

## PSALM 81

Verse 3 of Psalm 81 indicates that this song was used on the occasion of one of the three annual religious festivals in Israel. Because of the mention of Joseph in verse 5, some scholars say that it was written in the north during the period of the separate kingdom of Israel (922-722 B.C.).

The psalm divides into two parts, with the break at verse 5. Exhortations to praise and the occasion of the psalm fill the first four and one-half verses. Beginning with *I* at the end of verse 5 and continuing to the end of the psalm, the poem is in oracular form. That is, the psalmist writes as if God were speaking. Notice the first person singular pronouns which, in the context, must be God and not man speaking.

Like Psalm 8, this psalm is set to the "Gittith." No certain sense can be made of the expression, although some connect it with a person or event of the town of Gath. Five imperative verbs enjoining the people to celebrate the feast mark the opening three verses. In this respect the psalm is in the praise category and is very much like Psalm 111 and onward, only this psalm has no "hallelujah" in it.

More is said in Psalm 150 about the musical instruments. For now, note what they are and imagine the sound they might produce. The stringed instruments were strummed, not played with a bow. The timbrel is a small drum. The trumpet (v. 3) may or may not have been part of the orchestra. Numbers 10:10 states that the trumpet should summon the worshipers, much as it will summon the dead and the living believers at the rapture (1 Th 4:16).

Since they were on a lunar calendar, the festivals coincided with the moon phases. So the new moon is the first of the month. The parallel word in verse 3 occurs only this one time in the Bible. The King James Version uses "the time appointed," while most modern versions use "new moon."

The statute and ordinance to which the psalmist refers in verses 4-5 are in Exodus 23:14-19 and other places where these liturgical details are spelled out. Although some argue for the Feast of Tabernacles, verse 5 points rather to the Passover feast. The psalm is more concerned with the deliverance from Egypt than with thanksgiving for an abundant harvest.

Some question arises as to the division of the psalm. Verse 5*b* was put in the latter part, but some would include that line with the former. If that is so, then the psalmist and not God speaks in verse 5*b*. He is confessing that he hears an unknown language, the language of God. In the other interpretation, God is speaking and declaring that He hears a foreign language, perhaps the Egyptian of His people's oppressors. Yet another minor question arises as to whether this is a language He does not know or the language of a people He does not know, that is, know in the sense of election and love. God only hears those who belong to Him and who come in Jesus' name.

All commentators argue that at least by verse 6 the oracle has begun, and these are the words of God as He recites His mighty acts on behalf of Israel. Verse 6 refers to the labor forced on the Israelites by the Egyptians.

As the psalmist traces the Exodus he passes quickly to the wilderness trials which tested the wanderers' mettle. Especially did the showdown at Meribah, recorded in Exodus 17: 6-7, serve to establish Israel's absolute dependence on their delivering God. A "selah" closes this section. Verse 7 introduces God's exhortation to the people. Usually in these psalms man seeks God's ear, but the reverse is true in verse 8. The uniqueness of Israel's religion was its tenet of absolute monotheism, a truth introduced here, as it is in Deuteronomy 6:4, with a summons to attention.

Then verse 9 states in negative terms the most basic of the Ten Commandments. With the prohibition the psalmist recites again that most notable deliverance, the intervention into history which molded Israel into a nation, the Exodus from Egypt. The Passover celebration, to this day, focuses on the varied facets of that archetypal deliverance.

Having begun to recount the Exodus again, the psalm takes another negative turn in verse 11. From there to the end there is a logical development of ideas, ending positively with promises of abundance. Here is the development of ideas: God delivered His people (v. 10). They did not appreciate it but rebelled (v. 11). So God abandoned them to their own wills (v. 12). He wished they would return and obey (v. 13). If they would, God would punish their enemies (vv. 14-15) and bless them with the finest food (v. 16).

83

These few verses are a commentary on the lives of some Christians. Despite all that God has done to save us, we ignore Him. Though His only begotten Son gave His life, we refuse to yield our lives to His service. We also have the deaf ear, the stubborn heart, and the selfish counsel that characterized His people of old. How God wishes we would not grieve His Spirit! How He loves to bless us by eliminating our troubles and giving us spiritual wheat and honey! How He would feed and satisfy us! But we do not listen or walk in His ways. Or do we?

## PSALM 82

Psalm 82 easily falls into an outline which is roughly chiastic.

A  Statement that God is the Judge (v. 1)
  B  Statement of God the Judge (vv. 2-4)
  B  Judgment by the psalmist (vv. 5-7)
A  Prayer of the psalmist that God would judge (v. 8)

Whether verses 5-7 are the words of God or of the psalmist is the only question about this outline. That God, the Most High, is spoken of in the third person in verse 6 supports the suggested outline.

An even more major question is: Who are the gods of verses 1 and 6? Are they pagan deities or are they corrupt political figures? The Hebrew word *elohim* is used occasionally for human beings, as in Exodus 21:6. In John 10:34 Jesus cites verse 6 and applies it to the Jews who were about to stone Him for blasphemy.

Whether those among whom God judges are the heathen gods or local legislators, the point is that God is the Judge. Quite clearly, they are guilty of the abuses noted in the following verses. Verses 2-4 certainly fit better with the explanation that the gods are men, but verse 5 could easily describe dumb idols.

The crimes to be judged are generally in the area of social injustice. This theme is prominent in many of the prophets, especially Amos. Notice the number of times forms of the word "judge" occur in this psalm (vv. 1, 2, 3, 8). Because wicked men twist justice, God will judge them. The second charge (v. 2b) is tantamount to bribe-taking. These crooked elders gave preferential treatment to the rich and influential, while the weak, the orphans, the oppressed, and the destitute could hardly hope for a fair deal.

Verses 2-4 can be understood as the quotation of God's sentence against the gods. This interpretation is based on the use of the pronouns "you" and "them" (vv. 2, 4). With verse 5 the defendants are "they" not "you," so perhaps the speaker is the psalmist commenting on God's sentence. However, some argue that verse 5 describes the oppressed victims and not the abusive leaders.

Like Psalm 8, something of the dignity of man is asserted in verse 6. Because they are superior to the majority, better is expected of them. But since they sin they will die (v. 7).

The last verse is partly prayer, partly prediction. Notice the word "fall" (v. 7) and its opposite, "arise" (v. 8). Such plays on pairs of words are these ancient authors' poetical devices. Since rhyme and meter are all but absent, other characteristics mark their poetry. The prayer consists of two petitions: arise and judge. The prediction reflects the prophetic overtone of the whole poem in that God will inherit the nations. Since "nations" and "Gentiles" translate the same Hebrew word, this dimly anticipates the New Testament era when non-Jews will be part of God's Kingdom.

## PSALM 83

Psalm 83 is a complaint and a prayer of cursing. After one verse of invocation, seven verses of complaint follow. A "selah" closes that section. Then verses 9-17 constitute a series of maledictions, or imprecations, both big words for curses. The final verse (v. 18) gives the purpose for the curse, namely, to establish God's reputation.

As few other psalms, this one is filled with geographical and historical allusions which show at least that the author was a good student of the past. Not all of the places can be connected with recorded hostilities, but enough are clear to be impressive.

Three urgent pleas mark the summons to God in the opening verse. There is nothing of the flowery, exuberant address here. Nor are any of the particles of entreaty such as "please" present. It is a short verse, for the agonizing sufferer wants to get immediately to his subject.

Verses 2-8 simply recite the abuses in general terms. This section subdivides at verse 6, where the offending and offensive nations are specifically named. Each of the verses (2-5) contains two accusations against the warring heathen. Notice that the psalmist begins by calling them God's enemies, and later he comes around to telling what evil they intended against Israel.

As many can testify, one's closest enemies can be relatives or former friends. Protestant denominations and splits with-
m testify to this. So in ancient times the children of

Isaac were constantly at war with the children of Ishmael. Though both were descended from Abraham, the Edomites and the Israelites lived too close together to ever be friends. Also, note the children of Hagar (v. 6), the handmaid of Sarah and the mother of this hostile tribe living in Moab (cf. 1 Ch 5:10).

Gebal is a city north of Beirut and hence north of Tyre on the Mediterranean coast (cf. Jos 13:5; Eze 27:9). It is also called Byblos. Ammon is well known even to modern times since it serves as the capital of the Hashemite Kingdom of Jordan. However, Amalek is not a place but a people, roving nomads from the deserts east of the Jordan River (1 Sa 15:2).

Philistia is the enemy mentioned often in the times of the judges and the monarchy. Although Tyre was on good terms with Israel in the time of Solomon, the later prophets pronounce words of judgment on it (cf. Eze 27:3 ff.; Amos 1:9 ff.). Assyria, the giant that finally toppled the Northern Kingdom, is last in the list, having joined with the children of Lot. Remember that Lot was a nephew of Abraham and became the patriarch of a desert tribe.

The second major section of this psalm is marked by verbs of command. The curses are in typically Semitic style. Note especially the picturesque style of verses 13-16. At the top of the list is a plea to make these enumerated enemies like Midian. Gideon thoroughly routed the Midianites in the Esdralon Valley (Judg 7). Barak and Deborah won over Jabin, king of Hazor and his general Sisera, at the river Kishon (Judg 4-5). En-dor (v. 10) is near the river Kishon, but was not mentioned in the record of the Book of Judges. Oreb and Zeeb were Midianite princes whom Gideon's men killed at the end of a chase after the battle which at first was fought with only trumpets and torches. Zebah and Zalmunna are two other Midianite kings whom Gideon killed (Judg 8:21).

The citing of names stops (v. 13) and in its place begins a vivid and imaginative way to word curses. Above, the prayer was that the enemy would be like former victims; now the prayer is that they will be like certain useless by-products, dust, and stubble. Then the psalmist wants God to be like a consuming fire and destroy them like a burning forest. The next image (v. 15) is that God will blast them as in a storm.

The conclusion may begin with verse 16 because of the purpose clause inserted at the end of that verse. The reason for all this damnation is that God might be glorified, a purpose that is the essence of verse 18 as well.

It is hard to keep the glory of God in focus when overcome by anger. We ought to appeal to these imprecatory psalms most cautiously in order to avoid abusing the privilege of prayer and doing exactly what unbelievers do when they ask God to damn someone or something. If there is any other way we can make people know that God alone is the Most High above all the earth, then let us take it.


## PSALM 84

Like the psalms of ascent (120-34), Psalm 84 was probably sung by pilgrims making their way to one of the annual festivals in Jerusalem. The many rhymed versions of the psalm set to various tunes have contributed to its popularity. Here is the first stanza of one version:

> O Lord of Hosts, how lovely
>> The place where thou dost dwell!
> Thy tabernacles holy
>> In pleasantness excel.

My soul is longing, fainting,
Jehovah's courts to see;
My heart and flesh are crying,
O living God, for thee.

AUTHOR UNKNOWN

Many lovely pictures fill the psalm and speak both of the springtime of the year and the springtime in the believer's heart. But the devotion expressed here is rarely seen among Christians, who have the benefit of a fuller revelation and a clearer picture of what God has done for them through Christ Jesus.

Verse 1 sets the scene: a meditation on the glories and beauties of God's house. Then the psalmist puts into beautiful words (vv. 2-3) his own longing to be where God is. Having said it matter-of-factly and yet movingly (v. 2), he compares his experience to a bird finding a safe and suitable place to call home. Verse 3 does not speak of birds in the Temple but of contented pilgrims arriving at the sanctuary.

Verses 4-5 form a pair of beatific expressions describing the believer. In the former the worshiper is in God's house; in the latter his strength is *in* God while *in* his heart are the ways of God.

One of the routes to Jerusalem may be described in verse 6. The "ways" of the preceding verse prompted a reference to this incident or way station. "Baca" means "weeping" or "balsam trees" and may refer to an approach to Jerusalem from the west. The weeping may be for joy, or a highly stylized reference to rain, hinting that the occasion may be in the fall when the showers begin.

The psalm may be divided into three stanzas of four verses each, with a "selah" marking the division points. On that arrangement, verses 1-4 describe the psalmist's personal devotion; verses 5-8 depict the pilgrimage itself; and verses 9-12 form yet another expression of devotion. Notice the expression "LORD of hosts" (vv. 1, 3, 8, 12).

Verses 8-9 are actually prayers. The first is personal, the second for the anointed. Some would say this "messiah" is the king, others the high priest, and still others a reference to Christ. Another option is that the psalmist himself is an anointed functionary and this is a personal prayer, though it is in the third person. When one remembers that the Korahites were the gatekeepers of the Temple (1 Ch 26:1), this interpretation is especially fitting in the light of verse 10. This well-known verse is self-explanatory. One could only wish that it were the conviction of more of God's children.

Words of praise and exaltation fill verse 11 and then a benediction concludes the psalm. The word "blessed" occurs three times in the psalm, once in each stanza. It is not the usual Hebrew word for bless, the one used of God, but a broader word meaning "happy," a condition invariably brought on by close communion with God. The word opens Psalm 1 and is found at the close of Psalm 2. Blessed is the man that trusts in God!

# PSALM 85

Based on the forms of the verbs, Psalm 85 is in three parts. Verses 1-3 are praise and testimony of what God has done. Verses 4-7 are prayers mostly in the form of questions. Verses 8-13 are like an oracle predicting the bliss that will come upon his people. It is possible to read verses 1-3 as questions or as imperatives, thus making the first section essentially the same as the second, namely, prayer.

Mention of the captivity in verse 1 points to a post-exilic origin of this psalm. So do the later allusions to Isaiah and Zechariah. On the other hand, that may be merely a general term for trouble even as the psalm is full of unspecifics regarding sin and blessing.

Verses 1-3 consist of a series of six statements of what God has done. All are unspecific, but all are positive and evocative of thanksgiving. In a sense the logic is in reverse. First God must turn from His wrath (v. 3). This paves the way for the forgiveness of sins (v. 2) and in turn results in the return from captivity. The necessary item which must be understood is the repentance of the people.

Verse 4 begins the prayer section. Apparently some new cause for broken fellowship has arisen, and to this unspecified sin this psalm is directed.

Various uses of the root "turn" occur throughout this psalm. It describes the return from captivity (v. 1, "captivity" itself is built from the same root); God's change of attitude (v. 3); our conversion (v. 4); our requickening (v. 6); and our possible backsliding (v. 8). This flexible verb also characterizes Psalm 80.

Question marks distinguish the style in verses 5-6. They are rhetorical questions with the understood answer in the negative. The psalmist hopes that God's anger will not last indefinitely. He prays that God's people will not go unrevived or unrejoicing. Positive imperatives, as in verse 4, reappear in verse 7 to conclude this supplication section.

Verse 8 introduces what amounts to an oracle or prediction. It is a benevolent pronouncement with the anticipated accomplishment of bringing peace and instruction to the people. The content of the prospect is in verses 9-13. Certain expressions are like Isaiah (32:17; 45:8; 46:13) and Zechariah (2:5; 8:12; 9:10). The language is exalted with certain attributes or attitudes personified. Note the words "salvation, glory, mercy, truth, righteousness and peace" and what they do in verses 9-11. It is a beautiful picture, although hard to recreate visually. The source of all these blessings finally is mentioned in verse 12, which is a kind of summary note. "The LORD will give what is good" (NASB, RSV). Some would see here merely rain and subsequent agricultural abundance, but the tenor of the psalm is more exalted and prophetic.

All the virtues of verses 9-11 belong to and come from God. He alone is the Possessor and Giver of righteousness, salvation, truth, mercy, and peace.

## PSALM 86

Psalm 86 is a prayer of David, stated in the superscription. The contents support such a classification. The only evidence against this identification is the statement at the end of Psalm 72 that there the prayers of David are ended. However, there are many reasons to believe that the psalms are not in chronological order. Psalm 72 may be the latest in time, though far from the end of the Psalter.

Although the psalm is primarily a prayer, verses 8-13 constitute a hymn of praise in the middle of the psalm. The first prayer section (vv. 1-7) is positive, general, and optimistic. The second prayer section (vv. 14-17) is somewhat negative with its complaints about the enemy.

The psalm opens with a request for a hearing. The second half of verse 1 gives a reason why God should answer.
l times over this motif occurs: "Do this because . . ."

(cf. vv. 1, 2, 3, 4, 5, 7). In verse 1 the psalmist says he is poor and needy; in verse 2 he is godly and believing, and in verses 3 and 4 he is importunate. The petitions themselves are rather general: "preserve, save, have mercy, and make joyful."

Just one note on the choice of terms. The word "holy" (KJV) or "godly" (ASV, RSV) in verse 2 is built on the same root as the "merciful" (v. 3, KJV), "lovingkindness" (v. 5, ASV), or "steadfast love" (v. 5, RSV). It is the Hebrew word *hesed*, and Hasidic (pious) Jews use it to label themselves. Many English words are necessary to give all the shades of meaning, but basically it denotes faithfulness to promises. Just as God's covenant fidelity endures forever (Ps 136), so this ancient intercessor claims he has broken no vows but unswervingly maintained his devotion and trust.

One reason for the general terms used in this psalm by God's inspiring Spirit is to allow believers to use the psalms through centuries of changing circumstances. If people and places, events and times were too specific it might detract from an easy and immediately relevant application. Any Christian can quote this prayer and supply his own particulars as to troubles and wishes.

Verses 8-12 form a praise section (v. 11 is a petition for assistance in praise). Verse 8 is a strong monotheistic statement. The second half of the verse is difficult, as various translations will indicate by their divergence of opinion. Again, the shortest and most literal is as easily understood as those encumbered with verbiage: "There is nothing like your works."

Verse 9 may be Messianic insofar as it speaks of Gentiles (nations) coming to God. The frequent recurrence of this theme of the worldwide extension of God's Kingdom in the

Psalms should be no surprise since this is the book most often quoted in the New Testament.

The ideas of God's oneness and His wondrous works are reversed (v. 10) from what they were (v. 8). The hymn concludes with a promise of wholehearted, everlasting praise for deliverance from spiritual death.

The last four verses of the psalm are a mixture of complaint and prayer but include no imprecations. Verse 14 describes the evil intentions of the king's enemies. Notice the psalmist's diagnosis: their bad attitude comes from lack of God-consciousness. We might be more understanding and less vindictive if we saw those who hate us as spiritually lost men and as potentials for evangelism. Verse 15 may even be viewed as a prayer for the enemy as well as for the psalmist. The foes are again in view in the last verse (v. 17). Despite the hope that they will be shamed, there is still the prayer that they will recognize it is God doing good for the one who prays. Another probing question a Christian might ask himself: Why do I want God to do good for me? For personal comfort? Or for a testimony to unbelievers? Perhaps God would do more if we had His glory as our chief purpose.

## PSALM 87

Psalm 87 exalts Jerusalem, poetically called Zion, and the privilege of being one of its citizens. The holy city is best known as Jerusalem, but in many psalms the exalted name Zion occurs. Generally, spiritual aspects or concepts of that significant city are in view when this poetic name is used. A popular anthem is based on verse 3, but again the songwriter chose to call the city Zion rather than Jerusalem.

Verses 1-3 describe the city and God's love for it. The next three (4-6) speak of the cosmopolitan makeup of the worshipers there. The last verse, although difficult and elliptical, describes the program at Zion.

Verse 1, though very brief (because the title is considered the first half of the verse in the Hebrew Bible), makes the point that Jerusalem is located, by God's choice, in a high and separated or holy place. The psalmist goes on to state in verse 2 that it is loved more than any other city in the country. To cite the gates of the city is to use the part for the whole, a device used frequently in Hebrew literature. Then follows the well-known verse 3. Read Psalms 122, 125, 132, 133 and elsewhere to see some of the glorious things spoken of the city of God. Grandest of all descriptions is that given by John in Revelation of the New Jerusalem coming down from heaven (Rev 21:10—22:5).

Verses 4-6 are somewhat prophetic in that the worldwide acceptance of the Gospel is in view. The most hated enemies of the Jews are seen making their way to worship at Jerusalem. "Rahab" is a poetic term for Egypt, that arch-enemy to the southwest (cf. Is 30:7), and Babylon is the enemy to the northeast. Philistia and Tyre are geographically closer. Remember that Goliath was a Philistine, as were the enemies of Samson. The Philistines captured the Ark of the Covenant and later killed Saul and Jonathan. The mention of Tyre is reminiscent of the Messianic psalm (45:12). Ethiopia (Heb., *Cush*) is essentially the same as it is today, but at the time this psalm was written it had ascendancy over Egypt.

Just as the Gospel was for Jews first and then for Gentiles, so, in this psalm, no citizenship is superior to Zion and no birthplace more noble than Jerusalem. Often Jews make the best Christians. A "selah" ends this section as one did verse 3.

The last verse allows several translations. A literal but unintelligible rendering is: "And songs (or singers), like dances (or dancers), all my fountains are in you." If the first two elements are reversed and a copulative added, the verse makes good sense. I suggest: "Like dances and songs, all my fountains are in you." The King James Version follows the Greek rather than the Hebrew in translating "players on instruments."

Another question focuses on the "you" in verse 7. Is that the city of the Lord? Primarily it is the city, the source or fountain of the songs and dances. But of course the city is nothing without God. So the church building is nothing without the Lord of the Church. Where are our fountains?

## PSALM 88

Among the personal laments, Psalm 88 is one of the most discouraged and pathetic. It is the poetic groan of a man in extreme agony. Since he has no clear understanding of the afterlife, he is terror-stricken by the unknown. By contrast, Christian believers have no reason to fear the grave, and several reasons to welcome death, the chief one being their union with Christ.

The elaborate title demands some explanation. "Song," "Psalm" and "Maschil" (poem) all occur at the beginning to describe the work. Despite the frequent use of these various words, it is still impossible to consistently differentiate between them. Note that it is by or for the sons of Korah, the chief musician, and a certain Heman. Perhaps here is a good place to apply the theory that some of the psalm titles are not superscriptions to what follows but subscriptions to the preceding. Perhaps the part about the sons of Korah belongs with Psalm 87 and is in agreement with the superscription to that psalm. Two uncertain words, transliterated in the older version as "Mahalath Leannoth," come after the chief musician. The first looks like the word "dance" (cf. Ps 87:7), while the second is like the word "to answer." Both words, however, may be rendered, as in the Jerusalem Bible, "in sickness or suffering." Such an interpretation fits well with the contents of this depressing psalm. Ezrahite means "native born" and may refer to a non-Hebrew or original Canaanite.

No outline is readily evident in Psalm 88. Rather, there is a stream of prayerlike complaints centered on the themes of being forsaken by God and man, sickness, and imminent death.

Verses 1-2 form the invocation and address to God. Several modern translations unnecessarily change the meaning of the opening line from a suitably literal, "God of my salvation" to a prayer, "I call for help" (RSV; NEB). Even a second-best translation involving less emendation of the Hebrew text would read simply, "Save me."

Verse 3 begins the recital of the psalmist's problems, most of which speak of his nearness to death. This psalm is unique in having so many different words for grave and related concepts: the Hebrew *sheol* (grave, or hell) (v. 3); "pit" (v. 4); "the dead" (vv. 5, 10); and "the grave" (v. 5) (not the same Hebrew word *sheol;* cf. v. 11); verse 6 has "pit" again with the adjective "lowest" plus "dark places" (cf. v. 18) and "deeps"; verse 11 has "Destruction" (Heb., *abaddon* as in Rev 9:11); in verse 12 is an alternate form of the word "dark" and the poignant epithet, "the land of forgetfulness" (ASV).

97

The only hint at the reason for the trouble is in verses 7 and 16, but even then the specific cause is not given. The psalmist assumes that God is angry with him, but he arrives at no reason for that anger. Not all misfortune is judgment; it may be discipline or simply for God's glory. And certainly the God of all the earth will do right. The divine attributes of justice and mercy are obscured in this work.

A rather definite disbelief in the life after death or resurrection shows in verses 10-12. From the wording of the six questions in those verses the expected answers are "no." On the other hand, the poet may be like the preacher of the Book of Ecclesiastes who spells out the unbelieving position in detail and later presents his own conviction. In this case, verse 13 contains a glimmer of hope. "In the morning" may very well mean "after death," not merely the next day. That ray of hope is quickly snuffed out, however, by the continuing despondency of the rest of the psalm. Verse 14 contains two more discouragingly pessimistic questions. Then, to the end of the psalm, more complaints are directed Godward. In fact, the unpacified plaintiff begins to repeat himself. Note the similarity of verse 17 to 7, and of 18 to 8.

If the standard translation of verse 1a is correct, then let us meditate on that truth as well as on the truth of verse 13. But the Lord knows that the sentiment of the whole psalm sometimes best describes his wayward, shortsighted, impenitent, insensitive, and faithless children.

## PSALM 89

Psalm 89 is concerned with the Lord's covenant with David. Some of the promises of the middle section do not fit David himself but admirably suit the most notable Descendant in his dynasty, the Lord Jesus Christ. In Christ are fulfilled all the glorious promises to this ancient and godly monarch. Here is an outline of the psalm.

Introduction (vv. 1-2)
Restatement of the Davidic covenant (vv. 3-4)
Hymn to the Creator (vv. 5-18)
Promise to David (vv. 19-37)
Lamentation (vv. 38-45)
Reproaches by the nations (vv. 46-51)
Benediction (v. 52)

Without question the speaker of verses 1-2 is not the speaker of verses 3-4. In the introduction, the psalmist, perhaps the Ethan mentioned in the title (cf. 1 Ki 4:31), prefaces the psalm with words of praise for God's loving-kindness and faithfulness. The words "mercy" and "faithfulness" occur in verses 1 and 2.

Originally the covenant made to David came through the prophet Nathan, as recorded in 2 Samuel 7:12-17 (cf. Lk 1:33). The seed, of course, is the offspring, Christ being the ultimate Occupant of that throne. A "selah" appropriately concludes this little section even as other "selah's" occur at verses 37, 45, and 48.

Various allusions to creation power and sovereignty over the cosmos fill the hymn (vv. 5-18). Only at its end (vv. 15-18) is there something about God's human subjects, those on whose behalf His power is exercised. Notice the repetition of the themes of loving-kindness and faithfulness (vv. 8, 14).

The main part of the psalm (vv. 19-37) includes a number of eulogies and promises to David and his dynasty. In exalted language David is lauded (v. 19). The Hebrew root for "anointed" in verses 20, 38, and 51 is the same used for "Messiah." Among the promises are those of military success (vv. 22-23) and territorial expansion (v. 25). The king's piety is noted (v. 26).

With verse 27, the terminology becomes even more exalted. One suspects that the description fits only David's "greater Son." David was not the firstborn, but rather the last-born son of Jesse. Jesus was the only-born Son of God. Other superlatives such as highest (v. 27b, ASV; RSV) and the statement regarding the eternality of the reign are more descriptive of Christ and His Kingdom than of David. Strangely, no New Testament writer quotes this psalm and applies it to Christ, except perhaps for an allusion in Revelation 1:5-7.

Notice again the ideas of loving-kindness, covenant fidelity, and never-failing faithfulness in this section (vv. 28, 33, 34). The promises of the covenant are repeated in verses 35-37, with special stress on God's integrity in giving the covenant and on the everlasting quality of it.

Verses 38-45 almost seem foreign to the genre of the psalm. Lamentationlike, the psalmist looks at the discouraging present. He sees a kingdom which reflects only dimly the glorious past. Some commentators say the psalm was written during Solomon's reign, some during the divided kingdom period, and others during the exile. Judging from these verses alone, the situation is very bad. God is angry with His anointed (v. 38). His crown has been desecrated (v. 39). The buildings and bushes of the capital city are in ruins (v. 40), and the kingdom is at the disposal of murderous enemies (vv. 41-43). All that was beautiful and cherished has turned to shame (vv. 44-45).

The concluding prayer (vv. 46-51) is largely negative and complaining. It sounds like the plea of an exile. The covenant to David is remembered and appealed to (v. 49), not only in the historical past but also in the early part of this psalm. Bitterly the psalm closes with a view of the enemies of God shaming God's servants.

Book III within the Psalter closes with Psalm 89:52. The benediction applies to the entire book and not merely to this psalm.

## PSALM 90

"A prayer of Moses the man of God" is the title of Psalm 90. Most scholars agree that the archaic nature of the psalm's vocabulary and grammar support its early composition.

Psalm 90 ranks high on the list of well-known favorites. It is particularly fitting for funerals since the major teaching is the brevity and uncertainty of human life in contrast to God's eternal existence. Moses may be anticipating life after death in God's presence (vv. 3, 14). The general and elusive nature of most poetry disallows any certainty. "In the morning" (v. 6) may simply be the next day, or it may mean the day after death.

Evident in verses 1-2 is a beautiful chiasmus. Notice in the outline of these verses how the poet reverses direction in the middle and repeats himself with synonyms.

A Lord
   B You have been our dwelling place
      C From generation to generation
         D Before the mountains
            E Were brought forth
            E Or you formed
         D The earth and the world
      C From everlasting to everlasting
   B You are
A God

Having opened the psalm with this general statement of God's eternal nature, Moses then notes His sovereignty over the fortunes of men (v. 3). The words "turn" and "return" translate the same Hebrew verb for what is an obvious play on words (cf. v. 13). The verse may be speaking of death and resurrection. God turns man back to dust or slime (Anchor Bible), but one day He will command him to rise. Some men will sleep for thousands of years and others for but a few days. With God both spans of time are equally brief. Peter cited verse 4 when he spoke of the immanency of the return of Christ (2 Pe 3:8).

Then the focus of the psalm moves from the eternality of God to the finitude of man (vv. 5-6). Reflecting on the short life of desert grass, Moses likens man to the green blanket that thinly veils the sand for a brief period after a rare but abundant rainfall.

Verses 7-9, and 11 connect the shortness of human life to the anger of God. The implication is that if men did not sin they would live longer, maybe forever.

Perhaps the most frequently quoted verse is 10. In Hebrew, numbers are written the same as in modern English. It says seventy years and eighty years. In 1611 when the King James Version was translated, "score" was used for twenty, but that is not a literal translation of the original. The psalmist was remarkably accurate in putting at seventy the average age at death. Actually, only in modern Western countries has such a high average been achieved. And often those ten years from seventy to eighty are sad and hard because of decreasing strength and failing health.

The point made throughout the psalm is epitomized in verse 12. From this reflection on God's eternality and man's brevity comes the lesson: Learn to number your days. This

102

is an excellent prayer text for the lessons of self-discipline and goal-oriented living. But how few do it!

The application of the prayer of Moses, the man of God, continues (v. 13) with a second imperative: "Return, O LORD." The overtones of a lament echo in the words "How long?" But this request is against the background of all that precedes, especially the anger-provoking sins of God's people.

A flicker of belief in the afterlife may be seen in verse 14, depending on the meaning of the poetic terms. Even if Moses does not understand the resurrection, this verse at least expresses his desire for a long and happy earthly life.

Verse 15 is an interesting contrast. Moses asks that, for every day of affliction and for every year that witnesses evil, God give occasions to rejoice in their stead. This is especially meaningful in the light of the 400 years of oppression in Egypt and the forty years of agony in the desert of Sinai. Those who accept Christ later in life often testify that the few recent years of peace with God are worth more than all their pre-Christian decades.

The three sentiments of verses 16-17a express the truth of Romans 6:13b. Moses prays that God's work, glory, and pleasure might be evident not only to the people but also through them as well. Naomi, the feminine name meaning "pleasantness," is the root word behind the term "beauty" or "favor" (v. 17, ASV; RSV).

The psalm concludes with two almost identical phrases. It is a fine example of Hebrew repetition done here for stress and to seal the prayer of this ancient interceding sage.

# PSALM 91

Although Psalm 90 ranks high on the list of popular psalms, Psalm 91 is loved by even more people. It speaks of the security of trusting in God. Verses 1-2 constitute the introduction, while the central part of the psalm (vv. 3-13) speaks of the individual dangers from which the believer is protected. The last three verses (14-16) are a series of promises from God, who speaks in the first person.

Modern versions recast the first two verses in several different ways to overcome the difficulty of the changing persons. All these solutions are possible by adjusting the vowels of the Hebrew text, which were not part of the inspired original. So the New American Standard Bible has, "He who dwells." The Revised Standard Version and others have at the beginning of verse 2, "will say to the LORD, 'My refuge. . . .'" This confusion of speaker and addressee is not uncommon in Hebrew poetry. The overall teaching is not obscured by any of the translations. The truth is that whether you, I, or he, meaning the king or some other believer, dwells in the secret place of the Most High, we can say of the Lord, "He is my refuge and my fortress."

These two opening verses include four different names for the Deity: Most High (Heb., *Elyon*), Almighty (Heb., *Shaddai*), LORD (Heb., *Yahweh*), and God (Heb., *Elohim*).

Like most of the Old Testament, the psalm is written by someone with experience in desert life. The figures of secret place and shadow are particularly vivid against that background. In the desert you can see for miles, and a hiding place is hard to find. To the desert traveler the sun is his fiercest foe and a shady spot a most desired friend. God is such a shade as well as a military defense.

For the next eleven verses there is no inconsistency between speaker and addressee. The poet assures the believer of God's everlasting vigil over His people. Some Bible students understand this psalm to be written for and about the king of Israel, David. No superscription so limits the application.

The enemies against which God provides protection are of several sorts. The militaristic terms (vv. 4b, 5, 7) suggest protection in battle. Several phrases seem to refer to disease or plague (vv. 3b, 6, 10). Then there are the natural calamities, snakes and lions (v. 13), and finally the ever-present possibility of harmful accidents (vv. 3, 5b, 11, 12). Some interpreters see this explanation as too literal, and would rather understand the various ills as descriptions of human enemies.

The first threat is the bird-catcher's trap, the plain meaning of the poetic "snare of the fowler." Although no record exists of anyone using such a device to catch men, it is quite possible. The next enemy on the list is the deadly pestilence. Immediately the plagues of Egypt come to mind, especially since Moses recorded how his people were spared the worst of them (Ex 8:22).

Verse 4 interrupts the catalog of catastrophes by reasserting the sentiments of verse 1. God is pictured zoomorphically as a mother bird sheltering her chicks. No one says God has wings and feathers! The second image is reminiscent of the catalog of armor in Ephesians 6:14-17.

The point of verses 5-6 is not the terror or the arrow (which, incidentally, like the Hebrew are a nice pair of almost rhymed words), but that God cares for us night and day, in darkness and at noon. God never sleeps, and His watch is constant even when His servants sleep and cannot be consciously praying for safety.

105

Many military veterans have quoted verse 7, and such an application is entirely in order. However, it can have a much wider application, including deliverance from plague and other natural disasters as well as man-made ones. My wife and I think of this promise as we reflect on the hundreds of thousands of accident-free miles we have traveled. Of course, this is not to say unequivocally that everyone who has accidents or suffers disease is getting his just reward for wickedness.

Verse 9, like verse 4, is an interruption in the list of threats to life and safety. The "my" on "refuge" is difficult and translators have squirmed in various directions to make this verse fit the context. The King James Version added words to ease the situation. Others, such as the Revised Standard Version have simply changed the possessive pronoun to "your." Ugaritic studies have now shown that this latter option is possible since in that language the words for "my" and "thy" are often identical. Notice too that two of the titles for God from verses 1-2 are reused here.

Again (v. 10) the motif of protection from plague appears. A connecting particle joins verse 10 with the reasons found in verses 11-12. These are well-known verses because Satan cited them when he tempted Jesus in the wilderness. Also this is about the closest thing to a proof text for the belief in guardian angels. Two kinds of lions and two varieties of snakes conclude the list of threats in this psalm. Ultimate authority or victory is pictured as stepping on the vanquished. So the Messiah will tread on His enemies according to Isaiah 63:3 and Hebrews 2:8 (citing Ps 8:6).

Beginning with verse 14, God speaks to His faithful one, mentioning all the things He will do for him. Because the believer loves and knows God, God will repay him with this eightfold reward. He will deliver him and set him on high (v. 14). He will answer him, be with him in trouble, deliver him (translating a different Hebrew word than is in v. 14), and honor him (v. 15). He will give him a long earthly life plus salvation (v. 16). The last term implies everlasting life, the best and most enduring of all God's good gifts. But these blessings come only because the recipient knows and loves God. Both these requirements need underscoring since both are loaded with meaning far beyond their normal, modern use.

## PSALM 92

Several outlines could be fitted to Psalm 92, but the one which divides the psalm into three parts as follows is preferred.

Hymn to the Lord (vv. 1-5)
Judgment on the foolish wicked (vv. 6-9)
Personal testimony to God's goodness to His people (vv. 10-15)

The sections are very closely related, with a flow of ideas from one to the next. For instance, verse 5 ends on the note of the incomprehensibility of God's thoughts, and verse 6 takes up with the inability of the fool to understand. Or, verse 9 speaks of the destruction of the wicked, while verse 10 is the other side of that coin, the vindication of the righteous.

Taken as a whole, Psalm 92 falls in the category of a hymn. The title supports this classification: "A Psalm, a

107

Song for the Sabbath day" (NASB). Verses 1-4 are grammatically connected. It is good to do three things: to thank, to sing, and to show. In turn, we should show two things: God's daily loving-kindness and His nightly faithfulness. This demonstration should be accompanied by three musical instruments: a ten-stringed device, the psaltery, and the harp. Finally, the reason for this injunction to praise comes in verse 4, which is connected to the preceding verse with the key word "because" or "for." So this long sentence begins and ends with God's holy name.

Verses 4b-5 are exclamations about God's great works, with the Hebrew author using two different words for the three occurrences of the word "works."

As this section ends focusing on the incomprehensibility of God's thought, so the next begins with the finite understanding of a senseless and foolish mortal.

Verse 7 outlines the quick growth, the brief life, and the sudden death of evil men. Then, after the benedictionlike interruption (v. 8), they perish and are scattered. Though verse 8 breaks the idea flow from verses 7-9, it is not altogether unrelated. As the wicked are destroyed forever (v. 7) so the Lord is on high forever (v. 8). The grass springs up (v. 7), but God is on high (v. 8).

The psalmist's personal testimony begins at verse 10. Notice the personal pronouns (vv. 10, 11, 15). The interior verses of this section (12-14) speak more objectively of the success and fruitfulness of God's people.

This closing section contains a rich combination of very interesting figures or analogies. First is the confession of ox-like strength. Horns, then as now, are symbols of strength. The next figure is of anointing with oil. No liturgical or sacerdotal sense is necessary here. This is but a token of luxury of leisure comparable to a hot bath or a soft chair.

The imagery speaks of God's supply of strength and joy (cf. Ps 104:15).

The next verse (11) is a bit of what the Germans call *schadenfreude,* meaning "happiness at the grief of others." To see the enemy fall is a cause for joy.

An extended simile fills verses 12-14. First is the simple statement that the righteous are like palms or cedars, two of the stateliest trees in the Near East. According to the next verse, they are planted and grow in the Temple of the Lord, meaning of course that in the house of God, the Church, if you please, is found spiritual nourishment and holy maturity. Finally, though old, they are, like any good tree, very alive and productive.

The last verse uses yet another figure. God is a rock for shelter, defense, and stability. Unlike the workers of iniquity who have no righteousness, in God there is no unrighteousness. Can that be said of His people?

## PSALM 93

Psalm 93 is a short hymn exalting God's power over the raging sea. Verses 1-2 form the first thrust and the initial statement about God's majestic reign and everlasting strength. Verses 3-4 describe the roaring sea, and verse 5 concludes the poem with a reflection on God's perfections of truth and holiness.

Within the hymn are several fine illustrations of the features of Semitic poetry. Note the repetition of "is clothed" or "robed" (v. 1). In the original Hebrew these two identical words are back to back in the middle of the verse. The word "established" connects verses 1 and 2. Next is an excellent illustration of a staircase or progressive parallelism (v. 3). The scheme is ABC, ABD, ABE. Set up in poetry it might look like this:

> The floods have lifted up
> O Lord;
> The floods have lifted up
> their voice;
> The floods lift up
> their waves.

Verse 4 is not too dissimilar in its arrangement. Notice also that both verses 3 and 4 (ASV) contain the word "voice." Additional plays on words might be seen in verses 4-5 with "waters" (*mayim*), "sea" (*yam*), and "evermore" (*yamim*).

The poet who penned Psalm 93 offers a picture of a great and trustworthy Sovereign. Because of the connection between the words "reign" or "is king" (NEB) and "the Lord" (v. 1), some interpreters see here an enthronement festival where belief in God's rule over the created world was annually reasserted. Others see a foreshadowing of the Messiah where God the Father makes God the Son King (cf. Ps 2:6; 110:1). Still other commentators understand this as a song celebrating God's victory over the chaotic forces at the time of the creation. The girding then reflects the ancient sport of belt-wrestling (cf. Job 38:3).

No hint of polytheism is present, however. God is presented as the absolute Sovereign partaking of eternality while the created cosmos does not. God alone is everlasting. He made the world.

The ancient Israelites were not friendly with the sea. Even their directions were named so that north was to the left, south right, and west or the Mediterranean behind. Palestine has no natural harbors. Seagoing Hebrews were the exception to the rule. So the mysterious power and unharnessable might of the roaring ocean are all the more fearsome against this background. Their only hope was that God was stronger than the sea, higher than the waves, and more everlasting than the tides.

Having touched on God's glory, majesty, eternality, and power over the mightiest thing in creation, the sea, the psalmist concludes this hymn by asserting the truthfulness of God's word and His holiness. This climax to the song is also the conclusion to the argument. If God is stronger than anything He made, will He not be truthful? If He is greater than the sea, will He not be holy? The very last line is a strong, affirmative answer to those implied questions. Yes, the LORD is and will be so forever.


## PSALM 94


Several themes are prominent in Psalm 94. The most common is lament over the present success of the wicked and the misfortune of the good. Also present are the motifs of prayer for vengeance, imprecation, trust, and praise. The very title given to God in the opening verse sets the tenor of the entire psalm. He is the God of vengeance. Verses 1-2 constitute the invocation. God is summoned to take His seat at the bar of holy justice and render to the proud their just rewards.

The first lamentation part of the psalm is in verses 3-7. The characteristic question, "How long?" prefaces this series of complaints. The charges against the wicked vary from general accusations regarding their success (v. 3) to specific

111

sins and attitudes. In summary, their wrongs boil down to violence and pride; violence in oppression and murder (vv. 5-6), pride in boasting (v. 4), and insult (v. 7).

It is clearly against the background of verse 7 that verse 8 admonishes the wicked to wise up and get smart. Notice the device of the rhetorical questions through this psalm (vv. 3, 8, 9, 10, 16, 20).

In a sense the questions are really answers. So verses 9-10 are the answers to the sorry picture painted in verses 4-7. Yes, God can hear. Yes, He can see. Yes, He will discipline and correct. For God not only hears their words and sees their actions but also even knows their thoughts. Then verse 11*b* serves as a sort of postscript: "By the way, those thoughts are vain."

Though verses 12-13 are like a benediction of a different sort than the preceding, they nevertheless are connected by the key words "chasten" and "teach."

Through verse 15 the felicitous state of the vindicated righteous is described. Among the benefits of a chastened and God-taught man are rest and the assurance of not being forsaken. Couched in verse 13 is also the joy of seeing the wicked fall into his grave. The promise of verse 15 makes better sense when read with verse 20, where the wicked have control of the courts and decree unjust laws to their own benefit. But justice again returns to the control of the righteous (v. 15).

The questions of verse 16 introduce the first part of the psalmist's testimony (vv. 17-19). The questions and the complaint of verses 20-21 introduce the second part of that personal testimony (v. 22). But even those words of praise are colored by complaint and vindictiveness. His God is the God who rises against evildoers and stands in opposition to workers of iniquity. God is the high tower (ASV) and rock of refuge from those bloody men who conspire to kill him.

The sentiments of verses 17-19 are very tender. Here is a picture of a man on intimate terms with his Lord. He understands that just as God knows the inward thoughts of unrighteous men (v. 11), so God knows his personal integrity.

Although at the end of the psalm the righteous are vindicated, it is on a somewhat negative note. Three separate statements of judgment constitute the closing verse (v. 23) and focus (as did v. 1) on God the Avenger. The same God offers both refuge and revenge. Which do we deserve? Which do we have?

## PSALM 95

Psalm 95 has two distinct parts. Verses 1-7a are praise, while verses 7b-11 are exhortation. The first part can be subdivided into two strophes, with the break after verse 5. Notice how both verses 1 and 6 begin with the admonition, "come." Then both verses 3 and 7 start with a "for" and give the reason the worshiper should come. The latter part of the psalm is familiar to Christians because it appears in Hebrews 3:7b-11 verbatim (cf. also Heb 3:15; 4:3-4, 7). An additional connection to the New Testament may be the mention of God the rock (v. 1b). Paul identified that wilderness rock from which water miraculously came as Christ (1 Co 10:4).

The first part of the psalm is a fine call to worship and is often used for that liturgical purpose. Although it is not evident in any English translation, the two words for "let us sing" and "let us make a joyful noise" sound alike in Hebrew.

113

Elsewhere God is called a rock (e.g., Deu 32:4, 15, 18, 30, 31). Because of the historical connection later in the psalm to the events of Exodus 17, that epithet was chosen. The term was carefully selected from several available synonyms. Just as Jesus (Mt 16:18) was careful to distinguish between small stones and a solid rock suitable for a building's foundation (cf. NASB marg. notes), so this word is almost parallel with mountain, crag, or natural fortress. From where this is written the Continental Divide is in view. Geologists who have analyzed these mountains say that some are solid granite and weigh billions of tons. Such is the nature of our God: immovable, impregnable, immense, unshakable, everlasting. "I will lift up my eyes unto the mountains" (Ps 121:1, ASV).

Verses 3-5 are a hymn, perhaps one of the "psalms" we are urged to bring (v. 2b). According to the opening statements, Yahweh is a great God, a great King, and is over all gods. This is not a confession of polytheism or even henotheism. But, in the light of the following verses, it is tantamount to a denial of any superhuman force besides God.

Two pairs of extremes make up verses 4-5. First, God is in control of the deep places of the earth, meaning the graves, the sea bottoms, or the valleys. Next, He is the Owner of the mountaintops. To the Palestinian the highest point was 9,232-foot Mount Hermon; the lowest, the surface of the Dead Sea, was almost 1,300 feet below the level of the Mediterranean. Explorers have found no deeper hole, but they have found the Himalayas rising more than 29,000 feet above the level of the ocean beach. Both extremes are made and controlled by God. The second contrasted areas are the sea and the dry land (v. 5).

The second strophe (vv. 6-7) is briefer than the former but contains the same basic elements: command to worship

114

and a reason for praise. As verses 3-7 spoke of God's transcendence and control of the cosmic, so verse 7 speaks of His immanence and His rule over His people.

The expression "hand" in verse 7 may be a highly poetic term for field, which would be parallel with pasture (cf. Jer 6:3 where the Hebrew word for "hand" was rendered "place" as early as 1611; Job 1:14, where all translate it "beside").

With verse 7*b*, the tenor of the psalm changes from worship to warning. Some Bibles give the Hebrew names of the two places while others translate the words. The episodes referred to are recorded in Exodus 17 and Numbers 20 (cf. Deu 6:16; 33:8; Ps 81:7; 106:32). The wandering Israelites complained about the lack of water, and Moses brought it from the rock at God's command. Verses 8-11 are the words of God to His people, both ancient (here in Ps 95) and modern (Heb 3-4).

The psalm ends on an unhappy note, but perhaps this is to impress on the reader God's demand for absolute obedience. No words of comfort insulate the end of the believer from the intended sting of discipline. No opportunity is made available to let the mind shift to neutral and so forget these strong words of warning. For the inspired interpretation of these events read the message of the apostle in Hebrews 3-4. "Let us, therefore, make every effort to enter that rest, so that no one will fall by following their example of disobedience" (Heb 4:11, NIV).

## PSALM 96

Another edition of Psalm 96 appears in 1 Chronicles 16: 23-33. According to that context the work was commissioned by David and executed by the sons of Asaph. It is a fine example of a worship hymn.

The thirteen verses divide neatly into four parts: verses 1-3 constitute a summons to praise; verses 4-6 assert God's uniqueness; verses 7-10 exhort to service; and verses 11-13 enjoin all creation to rejoice.

Verses 1-3 contain several imperative verbs. Three times the command "sing" occurs. The words "shew forth," incidentally, sound like the word "sing" in Hebrew. The worldwide scope of the psalm is noted as early as verse 3 where the saints are urged to spread the word of God's glorious works. Verses such as 3 are the missionary mandates of the Old Testament. Ancient Israel, like the modern Church, had the divinely given obligation to tell. And like the Great Commission (Mk 16:15), the specific command is to preach. The success of the mission is God's business.

In Psalm 95 the pattern was "come, sing, for" (Ps 95:1, 3, 6-7). Psalm 96 has an echo of that theme. The "for" occurs in verses 4, 5, and 13. "For great is the LORD. . . . For all the gods of the people are idols [nothings]" (RSV). Again, this is not a confession of imperfect monotheism but a denial that other gods exist. True, they exist as statues, but statues are mere wood or stone, not deity. The Hebrew language words for foolishness, vanity, emptiness, and evil constantly overlap in meaning.

God is everything idols are not. He is to be feared (v. 4). He created (v. 5). He is worthy of honor and majesty since He possesses strength and beauty (v. 6).

The psalmist returns to imperatives again (vv. 7-10). Just as the command to sing is three times over in the opening part of the psalm, so the command to bring or give occurs three times (vv. 7-8). An expression at the beginning of verse 9 is difficult. The King James Version has "in the beauty of holiness," while the New English Bible has "in the splendour of holiness." Most others have something like "in holy array." The Hebrew allows both meanings as well as others such as "with the beauty of holiness," meaning a pure heart or a guileless attitude. Compare verse 6 with Psalm 29:2, where a similar expression occurs.

As the close of the first section (v. 3) had a missionary injunction, so the last verse in this section (v. 10) commissions the worshipers to be evangelists also. It is a three-point message that we are to bear according to verse 10: Tell everybody God reigns, He created and sustains the world, and He will judge it with fairness in the end. Verse 2b contains the additional necessary part of the good news: "Show forth his salvation from day to day" (ASV).

The verbs of verses 11-12 are technically not imperatives but do serve as commands to the heavens, earth, sea, and fields. This subhuman, inanimate creation is to join the song of praise. The creation was cursed in the Fall (Gen 3:17-18). It shall be delivered in the end (Ro 8:20-22). So why should it not rejoice, exult and sing?

At the end comes the reason why all creation should praise God. In a beautiful staircase-type parallelism the truth is underscored. God is coming to judge the people of the world with righteousness and truth.

## PSALM 97

Psalm 97 is a hymn devoted to the Lord's power and dominion. Its first half especially is loaded with prophetic terms and apocalyptic language. Most Bible students agree that a major break comes after verse 6 and a minor one after verse

9. Verses 1-6 describe God in His cosmic rule. Verses 7-9 picture the true worshipers' glee when image worshipers are put to shame. The last three verses (10-12) focus on the vindication and preservation of the righteous.

The psalm opens with a command to the earth and the distant islands or coastlands to rejoice. This follows the opening statement and the reason why they should be glad: the Lord is King. Note that a similar command closes the psalm (v. 12*a*).

Verse 2 on is an extended theophany. God is described in terms of nature. The first line of verse 2 may hark back to the revelation of God on Mount Sinai. Righteousness and justice are concretized and made the foundation of His throne. That throne is actually not material either, but a way to attribute sovereignty and dominion to God.

Verses 3-4 may go together since they both refer to light. However, verse 3 may speak specifically of the pillar of fire that led the wandering Israelites through the desert; and the lightning (v. 4) to the manifestation on the mountain. Or, the fire (v. 3) may be the one that devoured Nadab and Abihu from their presumption (Lev 10:2), and the lightning (v. 4) any storm which evokes the fear of God.

Melting mountains, a familiar figure in the Old Testament (cf. Amos 9:5; Mic 1:4; Nah 1:5), may describe an earthquake, a landslide, a volcanic eruption, or a terrific rainstorm. This section concludes with a statement on the universality of general revelation. It is not unlike Psalm 19:1.

An anti-idolatry polemic appears (v. 7) in the form of a fervid wish that all idol-worshipers be put to shame. The second order is that all gods worship the true God. "Gods" may mean false deities or simply human leaders. Either explanation would fit here. The Greek translation has "angels."

Verse 8 depicts the true worshipers rejoicing over God's

judgment on the false. Then verse 9 forms a benediction to this little series of events and ties in with verse 7 on the note of God's superiority to other things that people worship.

The last three verses take up the theme of the bliss (v. 8) of the enlightened righteous. Actually, verse 10 begins with an exhortation to hate evil. The second two stichs of that verse probably refer directly to the preservation from evil and deliverance from its power.

The light and gladness of verses 11-12 were probably chosen to reflect those same words in the opening verses of the psalm. These ancient inspired writers were conscious of style and form. They knew they were writing poetry and this often-used device occurs again here. As verse 10 had opened with a command, so verse 12 ends with one. Here it is to give thanks at every remembrance of God's holiness. The Jerusalem Bible translation of this exhortation is quoteworthy: "Remember his holiness, and praise him!"


## PSALM 98

Psalm 98 is very similar to Psalm 96, with opening lines that are identical. Verse 7 is the same as 96:11; and the last verse like 96:13.

A happy psalm, it enjoins us to rejoice in God's manifold goodnesses. His triumphs are described generally in verses 1-3. Verses 4-6 contain a volley of praise, while the last three (7-9) show the whole creation accompanying the victory of God at the end of the world.

The new song contains references to old triumphs. First and most comprehensive is the statement that the Lord has done marvelous things. Perhaps all the plagues of Egypt are in the psalmist's mind. Then, more specifically, He saved by His right hand and His holy arm, both interesting metaphors. This may refer to the Exodus miracles of the Red Sea, the destruction of Sihon and Og, and attendant wonders.

The publication of God's saving and vindicating power is stressed (v. 2). Together with verse 3, this is the Evangel of the Old Testament. The Good News was that God existed and that He has saved His people. The additional New Testament message is that we may join His people by receiving Christ, His Son.

A second exhortation to praise comes in verse 4 and is repeated (v. 6). Various strummed and blown musical instruments are to be employed in this holy rejoicing before King Yahweh. Even inanimate creation is summoned in verses 7-8 to participate in this song. In highly imaginative style the roaring seas, the clapping waves, and the singing hills are a part of this symphony.

The climax is God coming to judge the world (v. 9). Involved in that administration of justice will be reward for the righteous and the condemnation of the wicked. In this happy psalm, however, no mention is made of the wicked. The psalm merely closes on the high note of anticipating God's equitable court at the end times.

## PSALM 99

Psalm 99 is one more in this short series of praise psalms (95-100). In this one, particular stress is laid on the holiness of God (vv. 3, 5, 9). Some divide the psalm on the basis of the occurrence of the word "holy." Three stanzas then are broken after verses 3 and 5. Others make just verse

5 the one major break since verses 5 and 9 are almost identical. Note the progression from God's transcendence and unreachability in verses 1-3, through His dealings with the nation as a whole (v. 4), to His special relationship of revelation through Moses, Aaron, and Samuel (vv. 6-8).

Verse 1 sets the regal tone that prevails through this psalm. The Lord is King. He sits on His throne between the cherubim, a word lifted right from the Hebrew because our language cannot translate it. They were the attendants of the Ark of the Covenant, covering the seat on that sacred box with outstretched wings (Ex 37:7-9).

After two more statements about God's greatness (v. 2) the order comes (v. 3) to all peoples that they should praise this holy God. Though holiness is a rather unknown and difficult-to-define quality to most modern people it had a real message to these ancient Semites who used it. The basic sense is separation. As it applies to God, it means He is separate from sin, sinners, imperfection of any kind, guilt, and even from the bad attitudes of prejudice, pride, and presumption. God is free from these many forms of vice, and He commands us to be the same.

"The king's strength" may be an epithet for God (v. 4). God loves justice. In the rest of the verse God is addressed in the second person. Verse 5 brings another command to worship (cf. v. 3) and also ends with "he is holy."

In the last stanza the subject is God's revealing Himself to men. Moses, Aaron, and Samuel had a unique privilege to communicate with God. But through the testimonies and statutes we all can hear God's will. Again, verse 8, like verse 4, addresses God as "you." This is direct praise of God's justice and mercy.

The psalm concludes with a third verse of admonition to praise. Rather than ending with a simple "He is holy," the last line spells out God's name more fully. The LORD our God is separate from the world locally (v. 2). He is separated from its injustice (v. 4) and gives revelation rather than needing to receive it. He is holy.

## PSALM 100

The fitting title to Psalm 100 indicates it is a psalm of thanksgiving or is to accompany a thank offering. It was probably sung by worshipers making their way into the Temple.

The psalm is very familiar, especially because of William Kethe's 1561 paraphrase set to the tune, "The Old Hundredth" by Louis Bourgeois.

> All people that on earth do dwell,
>     Sing to the LORD with cheerful voice;
> Him serve with fear, his praise forthtell,
>     Come ye before him and rejoice.
>
> The Lord ye know is God indeed;
>     Without our aid he did us make;
> We are his folk, he doth us feed,
>     And for his sheep he doth us take.
>
> O enter then his gates with praise,
>     Approach with joy his courts unto;
> Praise, laud, and bless his Name always,
>     For it is seemly so to do.
>
> For why? the Lord our God is good,
>     His mercy is for ever sure;
> His truth at all times firmly stood,
>     And shall from age to age endure.

Most of the verb forms are commands. The worshipers are charged to make a joyful noise, serve, come with singing, know, enter with praise, give thanks, and bless.

The psalm is universal. All lands are summoned to come and worship the Lord. God's loving-kindness is "for ever" to "all generations." The vocative (v. 1) may be all the earth rather than "all . . . lands." "Make a joyful noise" is a heavy translation for one Hebrew word. The suggestions of some modern translations convey the crispness of the command: "acclaim," (NEB; JB) or "hail" (Anchor Bible).

The psalmist is careful that the joy of worship be tempered with adequate reverence for the object of worship. So verse 3 serves to remind us of God's creative power and absolute sovereignty over us. But to do so, he chooses the figure of a shepherd and sheep, one of the more tender illustrations of His concern and care.

If any outline fits Psalm 100 it is A B A' B'. Verses 1-2 (the A in the outline) contain a series of three commands. So does verse 4 (the A'). Verse 3b (the B) has two statements regarding our finitude and dependence, while verse 5 (the B') mentions the everlastingness of God's attributes of love, mercy, and truth.

Verse 3 contains a problem. The written Hebrew has, "and not we ourselves" (KJV). The Hebrew read by the scribes was "and we are his" (RSV, et al.). Both make good sense and there is no certain way to resolve the problem.

Altogether this is a most pleasant hymn with which to conclude this second volume of comments on the Psalms. At Psalm 51 the never-failing covenant fidelity (Heb., $hese\underline{d}$) of God was in view (Ps 51:1). And here at the end that same comprehensive attribute is left for our comfort and admonition.

For the LORD is good;
   His *hesed* lasts forever,
   And his faithfulness for all generations.
Amen.